**Trust is like your next breath,
you do it without thinking!**

Dr. Mark D. White

Contents

Forwards by

Dr. Mark & Helen Duplantis

Dr. Jeff Jansen

Introduction
Endorsements

The foundations of life can take years to establish, but moments to destroy. But starting over is a choice in one second. Preventative maintenance is the planting of a seed to sprout a tree with roots running deep.

Dedicated

To the wonderful gifts
God has given me, my children.

**Seth, Jordan with Evangeline
and Anna Grace Thank you for the
privilege and experience of being a
Father and a Grandpa!**

**Proverbs 22:6
"Train up a child in the way he should
go: and when he is old, he will not
depart from it."**

**To all my friends who were listening to
me before I said anything and
understood me when I did not make
sense. You knew my heart and
embraced it. Thank you!**

Thank you, Nanette McDowell, Melissa Torres and Barbara Hickox for speaking my language of redneck! Your help in editing the content and investing your time and sacrifice will always be appreciated. You made the difference!

Unless otherwise stated, all Scriptures, quotations are taken from the King James Version of the Bible.

ISBN: 9781688302495
Copyright © 2019 by Mark D. White

Forward by Dr. Mark & Helen Duplantis

I have known Mark White for many years. He has ministered in my church on many occasions. His upbringing has been in ministry as his Dad was a Pastor. Mark has a unique way in ministering the Word of God with Signs and Wonders following everywhere he goes to minister in America and foreign countries.

Many miracles are evident, and many churches have benefitted from his ministry in many ways having long term effect and change for the better.

I would recommend any Pastor to invite him to their church to minister, because Mark will challenge your church in many ways for God's Kingdom to be exalted.

Mark's book "Foundational Roots Imparting Success," has deep insight from Gods Word that will take you into areas of thoughts. It will reside in your heart that will draw your understanding of God in ways you have never experienced before!

It is an honor to write this forward, for it is really a wonderful book. Especially for those that are struggling with applying Gods' Word to develop character in their daily lives.

Dr. Mark & Helen Duplantis
Apostle/Pastor/Teacher
Author of The Constitution for the House of God

Forward by Dr. Jeff Jansen

When I am interested in reading a new book, I have to ask myself several questions: Is the life of the author consistent with the message of the book I am reading? Is the person's ministry supportive of the declarations of the book I hold in my hands? If I cannot say yes to both of these questions, irregardless of the content I will pass on reading it.

In the Case of Foundational Roots Impart Success by Dr. Mark D. White, I can personally attest a positive yes to both of these questions. I have watched and witnessed the life of Mark for years now and not only is he anointed for ministry, but Mark carries a powerful miracle working anointing with a razor-sharp prophetic edge that sets him apart as unique and highly qualified.

The book you hold in your hands is not only a revelation that the Kingdom of God is here in power and we are here to be part of it as normal believers.

I love this book because it challenges us to reach higher for the deep things of God, and that it not only leaves us there but gives us a handle on how to apprehend it.

I love this book because it's a call to all for spiritual re-evaluation of how we have been doing things as the church. It's time to believe for more!

I love this book because of practical faith is testimony to the supernatural, but a guide to activating in your personal life and the lives of others.

I love this book because it declares without clearly presented as being anchored in the unseen realm while living in the natural realm. Once we open this door by faith with understanding we are standing on the launching pad for a rocket ride into the Glory realm!

I love this book because it leaves me hungry for more and not to settle for what I have as an international minister myself. I am always pushing myself into the deep and this book inspires me to go deeper.

I can assure you as you read this book your life will change, and this is why I can fully recommend it to you without reservation. Read it slowly and digest its content. The results, I believe, will be nothing less than Miraculous!

Dr. Jeff Jansen
Global Fire Ministries International
Senior Pastor Global Fire Church
Author of Glory Rising / Furious Sound of Glory / Enthroned

Endorsements:

From Apostle Jeannette Connell

In Marks new book, one will find the wisdom of God through instruction and life application within the pages of his book. Through the written transparency on how to raise up champions for the kingdom of God, parents will find hope in this challenging age of parenting. They will be encouraged that it is never too late to begin to instill the truth of God's Word within their child or grandchild.

Raising children can be very trying in each season of their natural and spiritual growth and development. I understand this very well, as my husband George and I have raised six children. But through the grace, love and mercy of our Lord Jesus Christ, parents are able to walk out the greatest and most rewarding calling they will ever have.

This book will aid in the victory that Jesus released to us from His written Word of valuable life instruction. It is easily understood with practical application and explanation that will bring a transformation in your sons and daughters. Those who apply wisdom to understanding in the pages of this book, will be rearing their seed to bear great fruit of integrity and Godly character of the nature of Jesus. This will cause them to be prepared to accomplish their purpose in the earth. Jesus said "Abide in Me, and I in you. As the branch cannot bear fruit of itself unless it abides in the vine, so neither can you bear fruit unless you abide in Me." John 15:4. I highly recommend this book to anyone who has the privilege of parenting.

Jeannette Connell
Founder/Apostle/Author/ Freedom Outpost Ministries / Troy, Missouri /Author of Spiritual Cleansing Getting to The Root / Spiritual Cleansing of the Bloodline / Spiritual Cleansing Handbook

From Dr. Albert Mark Hines, Sr.

I have known Dr. Mark D. White for 30 years plus. He's Caucasian, I'm African American. He's Mark White and I am Mark Hines, so we often refer to each other as Mark White and Mark Black. Cliché' (he's my brother from another mother).

Mark is not only my friend and brother in Christ, but he's also a family man and a man of integrity who lives what he preaches and is passionate about his relationship with the Lord, his ministry, his morals, values, and spiritual beliefs.

I personally have observed Dr. Mark White raise his children, as he is a firm believer in the scripture: Proverbs 22:6 "Train up a child in the way he should go and when he is old, he will not depart from it".
We all know that many times when our children grow up, they will veer from the path that they were brought up on when the training is there, they will eventually find their way back.

I definitely endorse this book that God has put in Dr. White's heart to write. I strongly encourage everyone who can and will to read this book, especially parents, parents to be, grandparents and guardians.

Dr. White, be of good courage, keep the faith and the tenacity that God has graced you with. I believe that this book is and will be a great blessing to many people, known and unknown. God bless you I love you!

In His Kingdom,

Dr. Albert Mark Hines, Sr.
Apostle, Pastor, and Teacher
Pilgrims Rest Baptist Church / Greenville, Ms.

From Pastor James Maddox

Dr. Mark White's latest book, Foundational Roots Impart Success, is an excellent road map for this generation's success!!! The biblical principles explained by Dr. White provide real truth and hope for a troubled world. This book should be shared with every youth group. It is both practical and biblical advice for parents as well as their children. Every truth is abundantly documented with scripture.

Pastors James and Christine Maddox
Straightway Christian Center / Columbia, Tn.

From Bishop Bennie Jones

I have known Mark White for close to 40 years of ministry and friendship. His life has exemplified that of a true prophet of God. In this book, Mark displays the basic truths of how to live a successful life as a Christian.

The wisdom and instruction in this material needs to be in the hands of every new convert to help them as they build a foundation for a life in Christ. It is my honor as a Spiritual father in Marks life, to recommend this book as a life changing resources for anyone who reads it with a hunger for right living.

Bishop Bennie Jones
Pastor Vision Revival Church / Start, Louisiana

From Apostle Melissa Torres

Mark's book "Foundational Roots Impart Success" is a great reminder to us all of the legacies we leave behind, whether it's on purpose or not. This book isn't just for parents but everyone wanting to make an impact on the world around them. Each chapter will challenge the reader to not only think about the spiritual foundation they have received from their parents but also the spiritual foundational we are leaving behind to those close to us.

Are we truly leaving behind a legacy that empowers this younger generation to choose God and walk with Him daily? Or is our relationship with the Lord so shallow that it doesn't impact anyone around us? As you read through Mark's book I know the Holy Spirit will begin to speak to your heart about the legacy you are leaving behind and challenge you to a more intimate relationship with Jesus.

Melissa Torres
Apostle/Prophet/Teacher
St. Louis New Testament Church / St. Louis, Missouri

From Prophet Marty Layton

Dr. Mark White is a great coach for living the life God has intended for you to live. In his new book "Foundational Roots" Dr. White reaches out directly to the reader and encourages them to apply biblical truths that will transform their walk with the Lord. This is a very practical manual that gets right to the point. Get ready for a wonderful adventure with good, humble & wise counsel! This is a great book! It's an easy read, it's like having a great conversation as you read.

Prophet Marty Layton
Lifepointe Church / Hendersonville, TN

Desire amplifies ability and discipline increases results.

Introduction:

In my book called Time the Unfound Friend, I emphasized the authority and influence of time being the most powerful force on earth, I have been in the ministry since I was 15, and now I am pushing 70. I find myself re-evaluating the relationship I have with my children. I pastored and traveled when I had two wonderful little boys. But I was gone a lot, studied a lot and sought God a lot, not realizing I at times neglected my most valuable possession; my two sons. I know the teaching of God first, then family then ministry. I can and cannot agree with that.

How can I seek first the kingdom (Matthew 6:33) and it not affect my family? The effect on my family was overwhelming in all my years of being a pastor's son and being in the ministry myself. The teaching of forsaking all is in line with what Jesus said to Peter of forsaking all and following him (Luke 18:28). I have heard all my life of why win the world and lose your own family.

I can rejoicingly celebrate that my sons are serving Jesus today. But I have a treasure that I call my next breath and that is my daughter. At the time of this writing, she is 16 and even more the joy of my life. After going through two teenagers and seeing them raised strict in church as was my upbringing. I have two great sons to be proud of, but the relationship is not where I want it to be. They have seen and even experienced some of the price of the ministry, but not always the benefits.

So, I sought the Holy Spirit to teach me what to do. I had gone camping and fishing with my daughter, which was great when she was young and amused by those things which I did with my sons. But the things of this earth that are needed to raise a leader are more than prayer, worship, and love. Relationship is the key to unlock the heart of one. The spirit of excellence, endurance and believing in one's self; these principals are seeds to plant and watch grow. Like the following chapters in this book, these principals I was taught as I was growing up a Pastors son, they will make a difference in your life and others.

As the Holy Spirit spoke to me, I began to see the necessity of making a disciple of my daughter. I needed the power of words to be planted in her subconscious, deep in her memory as the roots of a tree that would resist any storm. Around the world, children learn the language of their parents by repetition. The purpose of these phrases is the required language of Heaven. Learning to speak as we live on this earth, as though we were in the City of our God right now.

Phrases with repetition are a necessity as we started imparting with **Always Tell the Truth,** the truth is required to live in Heaven. Our desire was the setting a foundation which builds her character, her integrity, and her ability to make wise choices.

My life, hers and her brothers is a foundational standard required for leadership to the putting of seeds which will take root. This will grow us in Christ as we build a solid future with integrity.

I hope you enjoy what we share, for I know what is in the pages ahead will help your roots dig deep. These are just guidelines that may cross culture or traditions, but the truth will set you free. It is complicated and yet simple, I just want my children to be happy, complete, and in the perfect will of God. Abraham was described in this scripture.

> **Genesis 18:19 "For I know him, that he will command his children and his household after him, and they shall keep the way of the LORD, to do justice and judgment; that the LORD may bring upon Abraham that which he hath spoken of him."**

**A Spiritual or Natural Father
Imparts into their children and
causes the roots of reproduction to
go deep!**

Chapter 1

Always Tell the Truth!

There has never been a tree that can withstand the winds of a storm without the power and depth of its roots. What you are holding onto inside yourself, and no one else can see or hear is what causes you to be stronger than your moment or causes you to run from the battles of life.

With what is inside you is more destined than what others think and more committed than pain, shame or lack of gain or you hide in the shadows or stand as a wallflower.

To some, you may be weird or somewhat insane, but different has a purpose. I have found in my life the things that my natural father spoke into my life set me with a commitment to what was in me more than what was around me. These words that I am speaking into your life will change you forever. So, **Always tell the Truth!**

1

While my past gets smaller and my moment becomes a memory. My future and my destiny should be my priority. My dreams always need a pillow, but my nightmares thrive off fear.

So, to be stronger and last longer requires you to run to the battle and stare into the face of fear. Denial is not a place to hide nor is it a place to share; the shame of it all is useless unless you can embrace the truth.

You can stare in the mirror and not see the answer or the problem. The purpose of a mirror is to look forward not backward, for preparation and correction to be your best and accomplish your desires.

I have two wonderful sons and I have put in them some of the things that my dad put in me. The weeding process of my Dad's best wisdom was overlooked, and the strength of his wit was not always embraced. But there are certain things I will always cherish! Like never hang your wash out in public for all eyes to see.

If you are one that does not wash your clothes by hand and hang it outside on the clothesline to dry. You might not see the picture. But to help you see and understand. Whatever is unsettled in your life that is private, keep it private. Do not let the neighbors know what is going on in your life. If you do not listen to your critics, you will never be criticized.

You might say if you have nothing to hide, but all of us do. That is why we do not live and work naked in public. There is always something to hide, some things are personal and private. Raising children is a responsibility of what you do in private will become public. Establishing cultural roots and abilities can shape their lives as the scripture says to train up a child is developing the gifts God has put in them.

One of the things that I emphasized with my sons is "If you don't try, you have already failed." I made both of my sons take piano lessons for about 11 years. Both have the talent, but both had not the desire. See, what you feed grows and what you starve dies.

Desire amplifies ability and discipline increases results!

You may not see in yourself what others do, but if you can become a lover of truth you will hate a lie. So, as you begin to look in the mirror and see the need for change or you don't like what you see and know you need change. It is not as simple as the fairy tale of "mirror, mirror on the wall, who's the fairest of them all." The truth is what some do not want to face, and we change the external while many times hiding the internal. But God knows! The process of becoming a better father with my daughter than I was with my two sons became the cry of my heart.

There is 12 years difference between my youngest son and my daughter which opened my perception. From the time she began to talk and walk, most kids learn the word no. But I began to speak into her the phrase **"Always tell the truth"**. I did not teach this principle to my sons. O' they turned out ok, but I remember learning things that went on that I never knew.

Just like one son, hid his school lunch for almost a year. He hated ham sandwiches and in place of telling us. He hid them. We found a lot of sandwiches hidden with mold that were dried up later that year. It took a while, but we saw he did not want to tell us, because he knew times were hard. I did not punish him, for I totally agreed with him. Ham sandwiches every day got old.

Both of my parents grew up poor, and they instilled a concept of appreciation in what you have. When I was a little boy, we were taught to clean our plate, this seemed ok, till you get overweight. Because you have to fight a subconscious thought of leaving food on your plate. The same emphasis I imposed on my children of appreciating what you have. But, if you are full, you should stop; and not eat like it's your last meal. Cultures can override the truth in one's life unless you are in love with the truth. The Holy Spirit told me to love truth more than people. This helps keep you from being manipulated into lying. You never want to hurt feelings, but compromise is a sacrifice you do not want to make.

So, I began a quest of raising a little girl different than raising two little boys. I saw and experienced their teenage years. And wow, did I joke, or did I mean it at the time "If I had known that babies turned into teenagers, I would not have one." One of my sons was above average in size and I never noticed till after he grew up, he reminded me how he saw himself and how others treated him. I was guilty, I just loved him and wanted the best for him, but my love was not enough.

It is not always good that love is blind as the old saying goes. We must see beyond their eyes, to listen to what is not said is more important than we realize. But my love was not enough. I learned how your love is not to be heard or seen the same. Yes, there are four different types of love in Greek. But in life, there is only one. The one that communicates the heart. As a certain prophet went to heaven, Jesus asked him, did you learn how to love. I can love you with all my heart and still be selfish because my love is about me and not you. That is one reason grieving at the loss of a loved one can be very painful.

There was a song I loved in the '80s about seeing through the eyes of love, seeing yourself the way he (he being Jesus) does. His love is perfect, but my display is to be perfected and to endure the storms in life, the roots must go deep.

Commitment is not what I can get, but what I can be. That is one reason that God cannot lie, He is who he says he is, and He keeps his word. Commitment! To this very day, I still speak into my daughter's life this word of **"Always tell the truth."**

As she grew older, I came up with another phrase and another and another. These phrases are the chapters of this book for the purpose of you being who you are. Knowing your call and destiny, then doing the right thing for other people's lives is the fulfillment of purpose. To be the best can be a gift for some but the disciplined of others. So, look in the mirror and never apologize for being true to yourself.

In William Shakespeare's Hamlet, the statement is made, "To thy own self be true. Recognize that if you want something or don't want something. The power of choice is in you; you have the ability to think for yourself, shape your lifestyle and create your own tomorrow. I believe that God's hand can be upon you, but the power of choice is a force that comes from within you.

Being perfect is the process of being perfected. Even Jesus learned to be perfect by the things he suffered

(Hebrews 2:10). The cross was not the teacher. But life, the people and even circumstances with situations opened the door of the power of choice. The power of choice shaped Jesus response, his attitude, his expectancy.

In Psalms 138:8 the scriptures say that God is perfecting those things that concern you. But in the God-given ability of the power of choice, we find the influence from others wants to help make decisions for us. What is important is how we respond, which has more importance than what happens to us. You cannot be an overcomer without something to overcome. No matter what the situation, **Always tell the Truth!** God does not make you do anything; it is your choice. Everything about your life is shaping your eternity, your past, present, and future.

In Revelations chapter two it is said again and again to him that overcomes, receives the blessings of Heaven. Even in Matthew 5:48 God makes a seemingly ridiculous statement, "Be ye therefore perfect as I am perfect". Now how can I be like God, how can we be perfect?

Jesus overcame every temptation and his self-discipline was because his strength was in his prayer life. He prayed all night while others slept. No wonder he could sleep in a storm, his roots were deep in a relationship with his father and the Holy Spirit anointed Jesus in ways we too, need to learn.

So, let us start with the responsibility of truth. Because you must always tell the truth because all liars shall be cast into the lake of fire (Revelations 21:8). Then in Proverbs 6:17 the writer tells of one of seven things that God calls an abomination, one of which is lying. The benefits of always telling the truth are eternal. Muslims teach a certain thought called "Taqiyya" this is an Islamic juridical term whose shifting meaning relates to when a Muslim is allowed, under Sharia law, to lie. Meaning lying to an infidel (non-Muslim) is allowed and encouraged.

Deception is the root of all lies. So, truth is what the Holy Spirit is, He is called the Spirit of Truth and Jesus is the way, the truth, and the life. Lies destroy relationships and trust is hard to restore. So, can you see what it might take to be like God who is perfect in every way? The truth is the only option, God cannot lie is what Moses said in the book of Numbers 23:19 and in 1 Samuel 15:29 also with Hebrews 6:18, It is impossible for God to lie. For God to perfect you, it goes to the root of who you are and what you will be. So, **"Always Tell the Truth."**

One of the most important things I can tell my children and tell you. "Love truth more than you love people." Remember the Holy Spirit is the Spirit of Truth. Again, I say; Love Truth more than you love people, for if you love people more than you love truth, you will compromise and give place to deception which is a lie.

Your life is based on what you love, not who! Remember what you compromise to get you will ultimately lose. In 1 John 4:17-18 "Herein is our love made perfect, that we may have boldness in the day of judgment: because as he is, so are we in this world. 18 There is no fear in love, but perfect love cast out all fear: because fear hath torment. He that yields to fear is not made perfect in love."

Life is full of opportunities and with that comes responsibilities. It is like a garden, you plant it, but if you do not watch over it, weeds will start to grow and that hinders and restrains the harvest you expected. The same principals in life as stated in Chapter Six: To Your Own Self Be True. In my book, the Power of Choice many relevant truths are applied in growth, change, and lasting results. You are sovereign, God created you in His image and that is inside out, not so much outside in. So, **"Always Tell the Truth."**

Jesus said in John 14:6 "Jesus said, I am the way, the truth, and the life: no man cometh unto the Father, but by me." Living in truth is not denial, and that is not the river in Egypt. But to your own self be true is a priority. If you live hating lies, this helps build in yourself the love for the truth.

Even Jesus hated the sin of iniquity or lawlessness in Hebrews 1:9. It is easier to love truth if you love the presence of God. Even the Holy Spirit is called the Spirit of Truth (John 16:13). The Spirit of God told me to love truth more than I love people. God is love and cannot lie. So, be the individual who never wants to offend the Holy Spirit in any way. **"Always Tell the Truth."**

I was asked when sin starts in a child, so here is a thought. In Ephesians 5:27 tells us without spot, wrinkle or blemish is what Jesus is looking for. So, he also said we must enter the kingdom of God as a little child in Matthew 18:3. The question is, would a sin-filled child be the example Jesus refers to? No! Sin does not start in a newborn child. Adam and Eve were sinless until the eating of the fruit from the Tree of Knowledge of Good and Evil that God told them not to touch.

When children partake in the fruit of others that being the knowledge of good and evil by influence, then it temptation becomes a choice. At that point is the age of accountability taking effect, and this happens upon culture, environment, and influence. That is why training up a child in the way they should go is a major important issue (Proverbs 22:6).

Developing wisdom in a child's choice is shaping their will. Some will adapt to following blindly and some will lead stubbornly. It's when the line drawn in the sand is crossed as illustrated as Jesus did when the men wanted to stone the woman in John 8:3-11.

Reflection of the past takes hold to shape the present. Sand makes glass and what's behind glass gives a reflection of the present. We are held accountable for our choices, and that is the line. Hosea 4:6 says we perish for lack of knowledge. If we are not growing in knowledge, this hinders integrity and truth suppressed is the foundation of sin. Remember in Revelations 21:8 the prophet speaks that "all liars shall have their place in the lake of fire. Never lie to yourself, to your own self be true. For if a person will lie to themselves, they will begin to lie to everyone else. So, **"Always Tell the Truth!"**
God is more than love, He is Truth!

Chapter 2

Love is Considerate!

Romans 12:9 *"Let* love be without dissimulation (do not hide your love). Abhor (hate) that which is evil; cleave to that which is good." *"Be* kindly affectioned one to another with brotherly love; in honor preferring one another;"

Love is Considerate but it should also be based on Love your neighbor as you love yourself (Mark 12:31). This is the beginning of establishing confidence, faith, and trust which is required to not be intimidated or manipulated by others or situations. So, in the imparting and establishing a positive subconscious character in my daughter's mind and heart, there are key elements to be repeated again and again. As stated in chapter one; **Always tell the truth!**

The seed of thought is the fruit of one's life!
The definition of considerate is simply in the synonyms of attentive, concerned, thoughtful, cooperative, patient, unselfish, mindful and helpful to others. In this chapter of **Love is Considerate**, love

is the foundational root which makes a choice of investment.

How you respond is just as important as what happens in life. The purpose of these elements are to coincide into ones' thoughts, that the DNA of her heart to be as taught like Jesus. When I say DNA, that is not just genetics, but the Divine Nature of God (DNA) operating in her and through her. Which in her daily life allows her to impart unto others in making disciples herself.

The power and influence of love are in the immediate response, and reach beyond logic. When someone is hurting, the display of compassion is rooted in love. The expression of concern and involvement is because of love. Hatred has no compassion or concern of anyone except one's self. The timetable of involvement shifts to immediate from postponed to let me help or can I help because of love, love means I care!

Just last night I listened to her speak the order of the power elements as I asked her to share. The power elements are what I call the Foundational Roots as each chapter shares. The main emphasis of love is, in every second on earth lives are changed because of The Power of Love. No wars, not hatred but around the earth to love should be developing influence in every heart. All of humanity knows and has experienced and desired some type of love in their lives. Even in cultish or demonic teachings, the issue of servanthood is there, and the greatest servant are those that love to serve.

The teachings of Buddha have so many different emphases and like the New Age teachings, all have the emphasis of a Higher Power working in us. But there is only one name under Heaven where one can be saved and that is Jesus. I can teach my daughter everything about love, but really there is no love without Jesus. **For God is love & God is Considerate** (1 John 4:8).

Do you know what love is and if so, can you give as much love as you receive? Is there a way to increase its authority and influence in your life? The influence of love can be read on a face, displayed in an action and received in a glance. Body language is somewhat the expression of what is inside the makeup of every individual. To hide one's heart is to cover up what we don't want others to know about. To experience the culture of Heaven is to start speaking the language of love because **Love is Considerate.**

Now there is always excuses and logical reasons some may use to try to excuse themselves from giving love or walking in it. But the one thing about the nature of God is expressed in Galatians 6:7 "God is not mocked or taken lightly, what you sow, or plant or display is what you will reap or receive back. Words, Attitude, and Actions are all seeds planted in life as you release them. In the world of self-worship, it is called karma or yin yang. This principle may come from heathen teachings or cults, but the principle of love is the same around the world. Even as Jesus said "Give and it shall be given, press down, shaken together and running over shall men give back unto you. Your words and actions are spiritual.

When love is more than a feeling it becomes an introverted attitude of action. It becomes a purpose of pursuit. As this is the second source of success I have put in my daughter. The principle and teaching of **"Love is Considerate"** links up with what you sow is what you reap. Just to put in simplistic terms, the seed you plant is the harvest you reap. I had a friend years ago who gave me a gift that had these words on it.

> "A friend is one to whom one may pour out all the contents of one's heart, chaff and grain together, knowing that the gentlest of hands will take and sift it, keep what is worth keeping and with a breath of kindness blow the rest away.

My friend died soon after, and I have kept those words hanging on my wall remembering her influence in my life. For she walked in love and was always considerate.

Many do not think they can love some people, but if you don't try you have already failed. Since God is Love 1 John 4:8 says, there is a principle that Jesus spoke of that is shared in Acts 20:35. *It is more blessed to give than to receive.* This one statement is the basest of conscience that I want you to understand. If **love is considerate**, then this is part of the culture of Heaven. Like the way, I was raised as a child and to teach my own children the influence of southern hospitality or the culture of the southern United States. It's called being a gentleman or being a lady, which are principals of excellence. Preferring others is a public display that Love is Considerate!

Things like opening a door for a lady or female gender. No exception for the wannabe females either. I can be considerate in a lot of applications from different cultures around the world. In some Asian countries, the honor the elderly receive is an application of **Love is Considerate**. In any relationship, I have always equated that love and respect were on the same level. With a lot of love comes a lot of respect and when there is little love, you will see that little respect comes when there are disagreements.

It is hard to comprehend how someone says they love you and then talk to you with no respect. Love and respect are the balance of life. They co-exist as one. Little love will open the door for little respect. A lot of love opens the door to a lot of respect to be opened wide. Even Jesus said; How can you say you love me and do not the things I say (John 14:15)?

But honor is preferential treatment and like giving honor to whom honor is due as stated in Romans 13:7 "Render therefore to all their dues: tribute to whom tribute is due; custom to whom custom; fear to whom fear; honor to whom honor." There is so much in this life to learn, it is important that our priorities are what we focus on, as we learn the culture and language of Heaven. This requires applying the principals and even the commands of Jesus to love your neighbor as you love yourself in Mark 12:33.

In Ephesians 6:2 Paul the servant of God says to honor your father and mother that it may go well with you. Today many nursing homes are prisons to parents which have been discarded, not honored or respected, but forgotten. Honor should be a fruit of love, not the type of love that has been based on what I can get, instead of what I can give. I remind you of what Apostle Paul writes that Jesus said: "that it is more blessed to give than to receive (Acts 20:35)." The issue is: what defines love to you?

Love is Considerate is what is explained in 1 Corinthians 13:1-8 in the Amplified Bible which is one of the best translation of these verses is really a great simplistic analogy of what love is;

If I speak with the tongues of men and of angels but have not love, then I have become only a noisy gong or a clanging cymbal [just an annoying distraction]. 2 And if I have the gift of prophecy [and speak a new message from God to the people], and understand all mysteries, and [possess] all knowledge; and if I have all [sufficient] faith so that I can remove mountains, but do not have love [reaching out to others], I am nothing. 3 If I give all my possessions to feed the poor, and if I surrender my body to be burned, but do not have love, it does me no good at all.

Love is patient, love is kind. It does not envy, it does not boast, it is not proud. 5It does not dishonor others, it is not self-seeking, it is not easily angered, it keeps no record of wrongs. 6Love does not delight in evil but rejoices with the truth. 7It always protects, always trusts, always hopes, always perseveres. 8Love never fails. But where there are prophecies, they will cease; where there are

19

tongues, they will be stilled; where there is knowledge, it will pass away.

This broad perspective is a simplistic application as stated in Jesus own words when He said in Matthew 25:40 "Verily I say unto you, inasmuch as ye have done it unto one of the least of these, ye have done it unto me." **Love is Considerate!** God is love is what 1 John 4:8 tells us, but then it tells us that we are made perfect with the power of love in 1 John 4:16-18. Being considerate is more than preferential treatment of others. The definition of considerate is "careful not to cause inconvenience or hurt to others". Some of the meanings of considerate can be put in some of these one words called synonyms:

> Being considerate is attentive · thoughtful · concerned · solicitous · mindful · heedful · obliging · accommodating · helpful · cooperative · patient · kind · kindly · decent · unselfish · compassionate · sympathetic · caring · charitable · altruistic · generous · polite · sensitive · civil · tactful · diplomatic

The power of love has a large responsibility and the display of what we give to others is co-dependent on what type of tree are we are. Trees of righteousness or unrighteousness. As stated in the beginning, in a storm the roots cause the tree to withstand the storms of life. For God to perfect those things that concern you as stated in Psalms 138:8 love is the roots that give life to destiny and the fulfillment of purpose. In 1 John 3:8 tells us that for this purpose came the son of God to destroy the works of the devil.

Jesus also said that "They will know you are my disciples because of your love". Life has expectancies generated by culture or what individuals think. The fear of offending someone can be stronger than the fear of pain! It is more manipulative and controlling based on the presumption of the possibility on what others are thinking. Confidence in the truth of your own heart matters most. Love is Considerate in many ways, preferring others is a great communication of respect and honor! **Love is Considerate!**

Philippians 4:13 says I can do all things through Christ who has given me the abilities of Heaven. You can do this because God believes in you as stated in Galatians 2:20 "We live by the faith of the Son of God, who loved us and gave himself for us." The unlimited ability of love is in every believer as stated in Romans 5:5 "And hope makes us not ashamed; because the love of God is shed abroad in our hearts by the Holy Ghost which is given unto us." Nothing is perfect until it is proven under pressure.

Being perfect is the process of being perfected. Jesus was pure his whole life, but really never became perfect till he passed every test. The last was overcoming rejection, when he cried out on the cross "My God, My God why have you forsaken me?" He did everything right his whole life and still, God turned His back on Jesus because God the father saw His only son that was perfect became sin, which is imperfect and flawed.

2 Corinthians 5:21 "For he hath made him to be sin for us, who knew no sin; that we might be made the righteousness of God in him." **Love is Considerate!** Jesus was made perfect when he overcame rejection from the one, he loved the most. But he stayed responsible and committed to his purpose and stayed on the cross and said, it is finished! You may not understand why Jesus cried out "My God, My God; why have you forsaken me?"

> In Matthew 27:45-46, it says, "Now from the sixth-hour darkness fell upon all the land until the ninth hour. 46And about the ninth hour Jesus cried out with a loud voice, saying, Eli, Eli, lama sabachthani? that is, My God, My God, why have you forsaken me?"

Recognize that what John 3:16 said is exactly what

God meant. John 3:16 - 17 "For God so loved the world, that he gave his only begotten Son, that whosoever believeth in him should not perish, but have everlasting life." 17 "For God sent not his Son into the world to condemn the world; but that the world through him might be saved." But this is the hard part of love, unconditional commitment.

Beyond feelings, beyond circumstances, no matter what love never stops. It is like light; it only stops and gives place to darkness is when the source of its power is disconnected. 1 John 4:7,8 "God is love and he that loves not is not in love with God," or 1 John 4:20 "If a man says, I love God and hates his brother, he is a liar: for he that loveth not his brother whom he hath seen, how can he love God whom he hath not seen?"

Love is just as important as the truth. You can have love without truth, as stated in 1 Corinthians 13:9 "For we know in part, and we prophesy in part." Knowing this is based on what we know versus what we see, you can have truth and still have bitterness or unforgiveness. When something is finished it is over and something new is started. To illustrate love is considerate. It is being considerate to share you are going to town, does anyone need anything, or I will be gone for a while, and if you need me call my cell phone. Communication is the amplification of **Love is Considerate**.

I taught my children, in reference to food or dessert of any kind, if you don't have enough to share don't bring it home. Somethings I was taught as a child has changed because the conscience of a nation has changed. But the principle of truth should never change based on the reaction of others. Principles are the roots of conscience and the strength of the tree, the distinction of identity, no matter the strength or duration of a storm.

Sharing is visible that you care. I love giving but I don't like giving when I know they are addicted to something and what they use my giving for is to feed their habit. Do not be an enabler in the destruction of someone's life, I am sorry, but a seed in poor soil gets a poor harvest. Understand the seed judges the soil. A seed is what you plant, the soil is where you plant it. Good seed in good soil is a great harvest, and good seed in poor soil is minimal.

Being raised in the culture of the south, we were raised to say yes sir or yes ma'am or no sir or no ma'am. This was a way of honor or being considerate. This was also my upbringing. Don't talk back to me was one of the issues of disrespect that would get your face slapped. I still remember my Dad saying on several occasions, "Don't talk to me that way with that look, boy!

Many times, I would try to freeze-frame my look and go to the closest mirror and try to see what he was seeing. It never did any good with trying to do that. Being Considerate is opening the door for others like it is being a Gentleman to open a door for a lady or the elderly. Love prefers, and **Love is Considerate!**

Defining love in an everyday life is a common denominator with the definitions attached with a question mark. But in the Greek language love is broken down in four areas. Agape', Phileo, Storge', Eros. Agape' is unconditional love, Phileo is friendship, Storge' is casual and Eros is erotic or physical. In relationships, we have three different types of friends. Close, Casual and Intimate. Close you choose, Casual the other party chooses, and Intimate is a gift from God. Usually, there is only a few who have lifelong friends which they can trust and know no matter what they will be there for you. Real friendship is not based on what I can get as much as how much I can give. But remember, **Love is Considerate** in many ways, preferring others is a great communication of respect and honor!

What you feed grows and what you starve dies!

Chapter 3

Be Responsible!

The next area of pursuit of impartation of what I believe God wanted me to train up a child in the way they should go, is to address their unseen character. Words, attitude and even actions can be planted as a seed in a mind. Being perfect is not in the vase, but what can be put in it. A seed comes in many ways and it can paint many pictures. The outcome of a seed is what kind of seed is it, what its identity by association, what is the long-term outcome.

What we see in the depth of our mind is what we live out in our body. That is one reason King David said to his son Solomon, "Guard your heart with all diligence," and "as a man thinks so is he" (Proverbs 23:7). A tree can surpass the depth of its roots with the height of its base and limbs, but it is the roots that keep the tree firmly stable in the midst of a storm. The pressure of life and the people in it can try to manipulate one to compromise integrity. To **Be Responsible** begins with one's self.

Proverbs 22:6 - Train up a child in the way he should go: and when he is old, he will not depart from it. Deuteronomy 11:19 - And ye shall teach them your children, speaking of them when thou sit in thine house, and when thou walk by the way, when thou lie down, and when thou rise up.

I have always called the first-born child the experimental child. Many a parent are learning to be a parent. But, at the expense of the first child which endures needless disciplines and corrections. The wisdom of the elderly exceeds the strength of the young; this also is known as the pen is mightier than the sword.

Knowledge can come from books, but wisdom comes from experience. Unusually the last child is called spoiled, the application of the child being raised can be different. It is at the expense of their siblings which wisdom and knowledge are gained. If we cannot learn from our past, we experiment with our future. It is true, faith is always spelled Risk!

When my sons were preteens, I was doing an extended meeting and I had my sons with me. As the Glory of God was moving, I started to let my sons lay hands on people and pray for them. They saw the power of God come through them and people being healed and falling out in the power of God. But all at once I saw my son lay hands on an individual and a demon manifested. My priority is to protect my sons as they learn by experience.

I crawled over the pews in a hurry to take my sons out of battle and to take their place. I knew the person would not have hurt either one of my sons consciously, but demons are the instigators of abortion which is the murder of the innocent. But it was neat that my sons carried the anointing to cast out a devil. So, **Be Responsible,** at that moment it was to protect my children. The ministry to people was important, but to protect my sons is always priority one.

Working with my daughter can be an experience of adjusting from raising my boys, because a girl's blueprint is different in many ways than raising boys. The teenage years take on a different approach, but the principles can still be applied the same. The promise of a future is built on self-worth and being responsible to one's self is as the famous play writer William Shakespeare statement of "To thy own self be true." Being a vessel of honor as stated in 2 Timothy 2:19-21 goes through a process of one's commitment to being fit for the masters use. Being responsible for one's self is integrity and being honest with your own self is integrity. So, **Be Responsible!**

Morals are issues of priority, like abortion has become a watered-down issue that is being impregnated into the hearts of today. The value of fun has taken the place of the preciousness of a child and responsibility is thrown out the window. Neglect of integrity can cause responsibility to lose priority because feelings take the place of the price of the moment. Many think it is ok to erase ones' memories like the wrong has not taken place. Only the blood of Jesus can remove our past.

Sin is sin, in one's thoughts or unconscientious actions. It is like the computer statement called Gil-Go, garbage in is garbage out. As Shakespeare said, "To be or not to be, that is the question." Many leaders or mentors want people to be accountable, but what is accountable is the exterior is what people see, compared to what the Holy Spirit sees and knows. In Philippians 3:13 Apostle Paul directs one to focus on destiny versus memories.

Be Responsible to your conscience. Never let submission exceed your conscience; Never! You might say "why," and the reason is, you alone are accountable before God. Submission to man should never exceed submission to the Holy Spirit and Gods Word the Bible! Your eternity is based on your relationship with God as your priority and not based on submission to man's government. Psalms 118:8

says, "It is better to trust in the Lord than to put confidence in man." Our time on earth is brief, but eternity is forever and ever. I love my daughter and two sons; I love family and friends, but as William Shakespeare says, "To thine own self be true."

Jesus said to, "love your neighbor as you love yourself," in Matthew 22:39. In all those whom I know and love, there is not one of them worth going to hell for. I do not have the ability to pay the price for other's sins or wrongdoings and neither do you! **Be Responsible** deals with truth, love, integrity, excellence and our stance or fortitude of life in our displayed attitude. If you don't try you have already failed, and failure is not how you start, but how you finish. **Privilege requires responsibility.**

There is such a depth of knowledge to cover in just being compassionate, responsible, and the big word is balance. But being responsible is not like this, "I shot an arrow into the air and where it fell, I know not where." Responsibility is not just the issue of what is right and wrong but having a plan or guidelines for accomplishments.

Albert Einstein said, "The world is a dangerous place, not because of those who do evil, but because of those who look on and do nothing" and in England, the statement was made in 1777 by Edmond Burke "All it takes for evil men to triumph is good men to do nothing." "To be or not to be, that is the question," as to the famous Shakespearean Quote –

In Shakespeare's Hamlet: "To be, or not to be, that is the question": Whether 'tis nobler in the mind to suffer. The slings and arrows of outrageous fortune, or to take arms against a sea of troubles. And by opposing end them. To die—to sleep!

We see the nations are fighting against nations and also race against race, as Jesus said would be one of the signs of the last days. But what are we doing to make a difference? Can blame be stretched from a small issue to a big lie? Yes, but the responsibility is still there. The Creator of Heaven and Earth said in Galatians 6:7 "Even God will not be taken lightly, what you sow is what you reap. Corruption leads to corruption and life breathes life. As President Harry S. Truman said, "The Buck Stops Here." Realize and take note of what Proverbs 29:2 says, "When the righteous are in authority, the people rejoice: but when the wicked bear rule, the people mourn".

To **Be Responsible** is as much for yourself as in being a leader in people's eyes. At the time of this writing, my daughter is 16 going on 20. I have tried to relay the message that being responsible is also being considerate because having fun as a teenager can get you in trouble. Well, balanced wisdom is weighed on the scales of consequences. Life is filled with opportunities as success takes hold of one's life privilege has responsibility.

What happens if light compromises with darkness? What happens if truth compromises with a lie? What happens if right compromises with wrong? What happens if integrity compromises with deception? What happens if health compromises with cancer? God does not compromise Himself to get you to love Him or receive His love, nor does He compromise the choices you make in life, creating for your future. God still never changes! He holds you responsible for what you do and what you are supposed to do.

I can remember my mother at different times would have my brothers and I go outside and scrub the pots, pans, and skillets with sand. Realize that friction can bring distinction and glass is made from sand, to create what we look into called a mirror. As we would scrub the skillets with sand, and this was done without soap and would clean the pots, pans, and skillets really well. Life is full of resistance, but you can use the moment to release things clinging onto you which should not be there, private or public. Even Jesus said we need to be purged and pruned to grow, John 15:2. So, no matter how rough it gets, **Be Responsible!** It is well worth it. Circumstances or habits should never control you.

Commitment can be challenged by feelings, because of principle and purpose commitment should never be compromised. What you compromise to get, you can ultimately lose. Purpose is the foundation of commitment if your commitment is tired or frustrated and wants to quit. Remind yourself of purpose which is the reason why there is a commitment.

Because if you don't remind yourself of why the commitment is important and just knowing that its Gods will, temptations still come to procrastinate, or it becomes not a priority. Feelings will try to manipulate you to submitting to a moment and not clinging to the reason of purpose! I John 3:8 tells us "For this purpose came the Son of God, to destroy the works of the devil!

The fulfillment of our salvation did not start with the stripes on Jesus back. It started when Jesus was born of a virgin. When Jesus was twelve years old, he was so into the pursuit of fulfilling the sound of heaven that called from within. He said, "I must be about my father's business". This alone was the open door to why he was born of a virgin and raised from the dead. This was done so that you could fulfill your purpose, see Jesus said: "the Kingdom of Heaven is within you (Luke 17:20-21)".

Knowing, that many are called, and few are chosen; has everything to do with: Can God trust you? Stay faithful in the little, so that Father God can reward you with much. Some plant, some water, and some reap the harvest. Who are you serving, yourself or God? **Be Responsible!** Your purpose is His will and like John the Baptist said, "He must increase, and I must decrease."

The pieces of a puzzle are made to make you seek the picture. Normally people start working with their borders and perimeters. But God works from the inside out as stated in Philippians 1:6 "Being confident of this very thing, that he which hath begun a good work in you will perform it until the day of Jesus Christ:"

The only limits we have are the ones we create because of fear and the fear of what others may think. Never neglect and postpone your God-given responsibility, discipline and diligence have great rewards. James 4:17 says "For those that know to do good and do not do it, it is sin." Sin is an issue that separates you from God's presence, and eternity is not a mystical delusion of someone's imagination; your tomorrow is todays accountability.

35

Having a complacent attitude or the actions of who cares, is being irresponsible. If you know to do good and you don't do it, you are still responsible. The abilities God has given you are for you to make a difference in people's life. Paul wrote this life changing statement, "I can do all things through Christ who gives me the ability" (Philippians 4:13). As, you find yourself growing in the ability of leadership, leading by example makes a difference in people's lives. Remember the only limits you have are the restraints of your thinking.

No matter your past situation or what we may try to use as excuses, you must be honest with yourself and know responsibility is your character and reputation of dependability. The Spirit of God told me back in 1986 "that if you live off of excuses, you can die because of the reasons." In the same time of prayer the Spirit of God told me "If Satan can manipulate your emotions, he will manipulate your lifestyle.

Be Responsible! "But you don't know how I feel or what I have been through," can be an excuse to stay the way you are. Again, I want you to realize that "if Satan can manipulate your emotions, he can manipulate your lifestyle." Addictions can rob you of wealth, health, joy and peace. I was raised to say, if you have nothing good to say, say nothing at all.

In teaching my daughter to drive I use the phrase of; "privilege and responsibility go together". I am raising her to be an adult, not a child that has a powerful force called a car, which is made available to her. Teaching accountability should be taught in all stages of life. Being accountable concerning your eternity, your family, your destiny, and your responsibility should have some type of priority. Accountability is minimal if there is no responsibility to your own conscience. Life is not always fair and not all individuals operate respectfully toward others.

One of the proofs of maturity is one's willingness to take responsibility toward humanity especially Christianity. People may prove by their age they are adults, but the proof of maturity is if one takes the responsibility life and eternity seriously.

Blaming others does not shift accountability and the word called accidents is not a justifiable excuse for what you did or didn't do. So, realize the privileges in your life, no matter what you have experienced. The power of privilege and responsibility go together. So, **Be Responsible!**

My grandmother told the story of a man in the town everyone hated. He cussed in public and always had a temper that would flare off over nothing. The man died and at the funeral, the invitation was given for a statement about the man. No one said a thing or moved to the front. We can never take responsibility for how others live or act. But how we respond is crucial in effecting what pattern others may follow. **Lead by example!**

But my grandmother stood up and said, "I loved to hear him whistle". This man could whistle all day long and it was so refreshing and enjoyable. Finding good in people is being responsible, critics think of no one but themselves, but when love speaks; it speaks well of others. So, to your own self be true. Let not anger or unforgiveness destroy your ability to love like Jesus or forgive others like Jesus. No one is worth going to hell over! **Be Responsible!** If you are wanting to live under an open Heaven and an open Heaven live through you, then remember that; **Privilege Requires Responsibility!**

Procrastinating responsibility causes one to miss the door of opportunity. mdw

Everything about tomorrow starts today!

God is not taken lightly; what you sow is what you reap. Galatians 6:7

Chapter 4

Have Integrity

Have Integrity! What is the definition of Integrity? Why does a person need it and what are the benefits of having it? The definition of integrity: the quality of being honest and having strong moral principles; moral uprightness; it is internal consistency or lack of corruption, the state of being whole and undivided. Knowing this definition,

I want you to realize that the measure one has is the measure one can give. No one can give what they do not have unless God moves on their behalf and changes one from inside out. This is like the faith in Romans 12:3, "God has given to every man the measure of faith."

Integrity is co-dependent upon choice, influence, nature, and desire. I have always considered a real liar is one who will lie to themselves and believe their own lies. It is a consumption of corruption that causes a person to sear their conscience to a point there is no guilt, remorse or fear in being deceptive. **Have Integrity!**

Relationships are the link in the chain of life. There is a pulling or pressure that comes on a young man and a young woman in life to influence their choices. The weakest link in this chain of life is compromise. Remember, that what you compromise to get you will ultimately lose.

It is amazing that in the culture of my upbringing, we were taught manners of consideration which in turn was to politely lie. Manners were considered to be polite and not offend. But, when food was served by a host, as a guest, you were to be considerate of what you received and compliment what was served.

Like, if a certain item had a bad taste and someone asked you how you liked it. You were taught to be polite and compliment instead of being honest and telling the host it was not what you preferred, or it tasted bad; but just say "No thank you, I am full," when really you wanted seconds or more of a certain dish. Being considerate is not being inconsiderate in telling the truth. See, timing is strategy and strategy is timing. This is a quandary, a hard spot to not offend or even lie to protect feelings, somethings are better left unsaid. But in being considerate, **Have Integrity!**

In my youth, oh' how I loved my Grandma! She could tell stories of experiences as a youth that held my total attention. Like the time of her and her younger brother and sister were coming home from school. There were no buses and the walk home was long. As the evening was taking place as the sun was setting. They could hear the howl of wolves deep into the woods. They knew time was slipping away and they had to hurry to keep away from the wolves. Darkness was setting in and the sound of the wolves was closer and closer. So, my grandma and her siblings crawled into a log that crossed a creek. She knew they had to protect themselves from the wolves.

The wolves came closer as the sun began to set, the hollowed log and a stick were the only things keeping the wolves at bay. Then out of nowhere the sound of a gun went off and the wolves began to scatter. Her Dad knew they were late in coming home, so he went looking for them. I'm sharing this story to help illustrate that integrity is protecting what you love. Just as stated in **Being Responsible** and **Love is Considerate. Having Integrity** is keeping your promise and doing everything you can to fulfill your word. Your priority is keeping your word, and when you say to someone that you will be there for them, you must do your best to keep your word. What you believe in you invest in, love will sacrifice to protect.

Your word is your bond. Commitment is the key to the depth of trust. Trust is like your next breath, you do it without thinking! I can remember the story of my Grandma as a little girl; she was running with a snake chasing her. Her dad yelling out "let go of the pole," which had a fish attached to it and she is yelling back, "No it is dinner!" As an example, God keeps His word and He cannot lie, neither should we ever lie. My Grandma made a promise to catch dinner and she was not willing to share with a snake. Keep your word if all possible, for in Psalms 15:1-5 it states in context that promotion into the higher places in God has to do with keeping your word.

Being raised by parents of who had experiences after experiences in life was so awesome. My Dad grew up a farmer's son and my mother was raised chopping and picking cotton. I remember once running to the house because a water moccasin was chasing us as kids. Being raised on a Louisiana Bayou called The Bonne Idee Bayou which was French for Good Idea were memories I will never forget. I loved to fish and even just watch the beauty of God's creation as the alligators, ducks, geese and snapping turtles were at my back door.

I remember my Dad sent me to town to get something for him and I had just caught a nice size catfish. So, I put the catfish on a stringer and left. After I got home, I went back to get my catch and was I ever surprised.

A water moccasin, also known as a cottonmouth, had swallowed over half of my catfish which was still attached to the stringer. The water moccasin being a poisonous snake forced me to help both meet Jesus with my shotgun. Shame, it was a nice size catfish too. Doing right still might seem wrong to some but to try to save the fish could have gotten me bit by the snake defending its dinner. So, realize that **Having Integrity** also is working with **Be Responsible** and **Always Telling the Truth.** The catfish did not volunteer to be the snakes' lunch. Don't volunteer to lie.

When you love truth more than you love people, you are a person of character! That is why God cannot lie. He has character, his moral compass always brings the heart of the matter to purity, righteousness, and truth. Romans 14:17 tells us that "For the kingdom of God is not meat and drink; but righteousness, and peace, and joy in the Holy Ghost." Your whole future is based on the seed of your today.

What are you planting in the depth of your soul, the mind of Christ or the corruption of this world? When the Apostle Paul said 2 Corinthians 6:17 "Wherefore come out from among them, and be ye separate, saith the Lord, and touch not the unclean *thing*; and I will receive you," this statement is instructions for preventative maintenance.

Abstinence is not based on where you go or what you do as much as, how you do it. Do you blend in or stand out? For years I was raised in more of I cannot do this, or I cannot do that. We could not go to movies; we were told Jesus would not come in there after you. We could not go bowling, play pool, etc. I thought this was holiness. Boy was I wrong and mislead.

The sincerity of the people I loved was there, but the error was too. My holiness and purity are based on integrity. Not deception of how you dress or where you don't go but still talked and acted like the world with a carnal mindset. Even in Romans 8:7 says that carnal Christians are the enemy of God. Carnal are those that live after the old nature of the sinful flesh and not the nature of your born-again spirit. **Have Integrity!**

By far, I am not perfect even though God is perfecting those things that concern me as stated in Psalms 138:8. But as stated in Chapter One: **Always Tell the Truth!** Is a standard, a root of strength to resist deception that some will come in your life as you grow older. People that easily lie will eventually easily believe a lie. God is love, but so much more than love, He is Truth. Psalm 18:30 As for God, his way is perfect: the word of the Lord is tried and proven. In Deuteronomy 32:4 "The Rock! His work is perfect, for all His ways are just; A God of faithfulness and without injustice, Righteous and upright is He.

Some things we have a desire to learn but if we are not willing to pay the price to learn, how can you accomplish your desires. Some would be so petty to say if God wanted me to have it; He would give it to me. That is an excuse used by those who have to deal with fear in flying in an airplane, "If God wanted me to fly, He would have given me wings." In Psalms 103:7 tells us that Moses knew God's ways, but Israel only knew Gods acts.

Psalms 75 says promotion comes from God, God knows your heart, He sees your ways, but He also knows His will for you. Hebrews 5:8-9 tells us that Jesus learned through suffering and that was before the cross, "Although He was a Son, He learned obedience from the things which He suffered. And having been made perfect, He became to all those who obey Him the source of eternal salvation."

To **Have Integrity** is what you develop inside your subconscious. That which you do without thinking. That which is who you are. Believing in yourself is based on what you know about yourself, what you think about yourself and what others expect out of you. See faith and fear are two powerful forces. Both have the ability to create something out of nothing and bring into existence that which does not exist. The power of the supernatural is as God spoke to Joshua in the book of Joshua 1:8 to meditate on the word of God day and night and then you will accomplish what you are called to.

The consistent planting of the word of God by meditating scriptures helps develop your life and character. This causes accomplishments which are seeds to grow a harvest of reaping for the rest of your life. This will be the depth of foundational roots that will secure your life in a storm to be strong and stable. There are no short cuts to diamonds, true pure diamonds are created or transformed from coal to the pressure of time into a most valuable stone. But then it is cut and shaped to fulfill the desire of the jeweler.

The Potter is God and we are the clay and He is shaping you as you work with Him in doing His will. He is working in you his goodwill and pleasure. He is training you for reigning, being a leader is not just a type A personality but a person that leads by example. How can you influence others at school when you are no different than anyone else?

The sports star might have skill but if he prefers others, they lead by example. Being truthful and honest is only part of what it takes to **Have Integrity**. I have taught my sons over and over this phrase, "If you don't try, you have already failed." Both of my sons have had 11 years of piano lessons. I had a standard, if you want to play soccer or baseball or football, you must play the piano, if you want to breathe you play the piano. They are both alive and good at what they do. Piano opened the door for both to play the guitar, drums, bass guitar, even a ukulele.

Music is not just reading notes, but ones innermost feelings can be expressed. It is said that those individuals which learn to play music instruments opens academic skills above average. The discipline of learning makes life a quest. Being good at Math is recognized as a benefit that music brings, so is reading music versus playing by ear, **Doing it right is Integrity.**

There is an old saying that gossip dies when it hits a wise person's ear. To **Have Integrity** you must make choices and you learn how you stand on issues which will affect who wants to be your friend.

> Psalms 15:1-4 Lord, who shall abide in thy tabernacle? who shall dwell in thy holy hill? 2 He that walketh uprightly, and worketh righteousness, and speaks the truth in his heart. 3 He that backbites not with his tongue, nor doeth evil to his neighbor, nor taketh up a reproach against his neighbor. 4 In whose eyes a vile person is contemned; but he honors them that fear the LORD. He that swears to his own hurt, and changes not.

Psalms 24:3-5 Who shall ascend into the hill of the LORD? or who shall stand in his holy place? 4 He that hath clean hands, and a pure heart; who hath not lifted up his soul unto vanity, nor sworn deceitfully. 5 He shall receive the blessing from the LORD, and righteousness from the God of his salvation.

As I stated in the beginning of this book about roots and foundations. It is imperative that you know what you know, and you believe what you believe. Being confused is based on fear versus trust and confidence in oneself. It is also important to root out the generational curses of your heritage. James 1:8 says that people that do not believe in what they believe in or they are like the wind. They change often on a subject because of being unsure about what they say or say they believe. I know this because of family and friends putting the pressure to conform to other's ideas and not one's own conscience.

Do not be double-minded. It is easier for God to speed things up than correct mistakes. My eternity is based on my conscience and my relationship with Jesus. When I am at the judgment seat, I will be judged for the choices I make, not what others make or try to make for me. See Jesus said in Matthew 5:8 that the pure in heart shall see God. Stability is Gods analogy of Abraham when God said I can trust him in

Genesis 18:19 "For I know him, that he will command his children and his household after him, and they shall keep the way of the LORD, to do justice and judgment; that the LORD may bring upon Abraham that which he hath spoken of him."

Running from a battle is running from victory. Running from what people say about you is running from vindication. Life is full of battles, but victories are only to those that stand on principles of truth, not parallels of people's opinion. You can run from battles but not the war of life. You can choose your battles, but not choose the war of life. Remember your eternity is based totally on you individually and what you believe, not what others think. So, when you have done all, stand your ground, because a smile from Heaven does not remove the frown of carnal men. **So, Have Integrity!**

Desire amplifies ability and discipline increases results.

Proverbs 13:20 "He that walketh with wise *men* shall be wise: but a companion of fools shall be destroyed."

The man that history calls Honest Abe is the 16th President of the United States of America. Abraham Lincoln created this code of conduct and I think it is worth you taking a look and apply in one's life.

Abraham Lincolns Code of Conduct

1. Be sure you put your feet in the right place, then stand firm.
2. Better to remain silent and be thought a fool than to speak out and remove all doubt.
3. The fact is, truth is your truest friend, no matter what the circumstances are.
4. Leave nothing for tomorrow which can be done today.
5. The way for a young man to rise is to improve himself every way he can, never suspecting that anybody wishes to hinder him.
6. Quarrel not at all. No man resolved to make the most of himself can spare time for personal contention.
7. By all means, don't say "if I can," say "I will.'
8. Let none falter who thinks he is right.
9. I say "try." If we never try, we shall never succeed.
10. Stand with anybody that stands right. Stand with him while he is right, and part with him when he goes wrong.

And in my words, **Have Integrity!** For in Mark 9:23 "Jesus said unto him, if thou canst believe, all things *are* possible to him that believeth." All receiving is based on believing! So, what are you expecting? As William Shakespeare said, "To thy own self be true."

**"A lie doesn't become truth,
Wrong doesn't become right
and evil doesn't become good
just because it's accepted by a majority."**

Booker T. Washington

If you live by excuses, you can die because of the reasons!

Chapter Five:

Pursue Excellence!

In the book of Matthew 5:48 Jesus said: "Be ye therefore perfect, even as your Father which is in heaven is perfect." Developing the language of Heaven is to pursue excellence. Being like God is never doing something with a halfway attitude toward accomplishment. I find myself working uphill in developing the attributes of excellence with consistency.

The demand of responsibility presses one into accountability.

Years ago, I had a good friend who would never go to bed without stacking his loose change. All dimes were stacked neatly, all quarters stacked, all nickels and even pennies were perfectly stacked. He was an average guy, but now he is a millionaire. What you do in private is what you will do in public.

"Be ye perfect, as I am perfect," are the attributes of a perfectionist which are not always the display of a personality trait. These are the developed, disciplined, and desired vision of an accomplishment type of person. In pursuing excellence, a perfectionist is not satisfied with just barely making it.

The word "pursue" means to set a direction of applications for results and accomplishments. The word "excellence" means it is a talent or quality which is beyond unusually good and thereby surpasses ordinary standards. The word "perfect" also is used as a standard of performance and measured comparison.

Setting standards and goals always requires a plan. Without a plan or a vision, a dream can fade, and a desire can falter. What is desired is acquired, and what you pursue you can do. But the height of accomplishment is better to set as with the distance of the moon, than just a mountain top or even the size of a molehill which will never get you off the ground. Aspire your desire, feed your fire, pursue what you cannot do and realize destiny is calling you. **Pursue Excellence!** Remember an idle mind is the devil's workshop.

The opposite of excellence can be defined as slothful, lazy, idle, inactive and indifferent. Excellence is akin (which means of similar character) to perfection. I can boldly say that the nature of God is of Excellence. To have excellence as part of one's nature is to develop the foundation of all the titles of the chapters in this book. **Always Tell the Truth, Love is**

Considerate, Be Responsible, Have Integrity, Pursue Excellence, To Your Own Self Be True, Control Your Attitude, and Being Safe is Wisdom. Repetition is impregnation. The seed of one's thoughts can grow to the point that out of the abundance of the heart your mouth speaks (Matthew 12:34).

Controlling your thoughts affects your subconscious. Proverbs 23:7 declares "For as one thinks, they display their heart." Overcoming your past and developing your future requires an overwhelming investment in oneself called education. Knowledge can set you on a path, but choices keep you committed.

The following statement will be repeated because of its relevance. "Be careful of your thoughts, for your thoughts become your words. Be careful of your words, for your words become your actions. Be careful of your actions, for your actions become your habits. Be careful of your habits for your habits become your character. Be careful of your character, for your character creates your future." (author unknown)

To Pursue Excellence, you have to develop a Spirit of Excellence. As shared in Philippians 1:10 Apostle Paul says "Ye may approve things that are excellent; that ye may be sincere and without offense till the day of Christ." In Proverbs 12:24 this statement is an eye-opener, "Diligent hands will rule, but laziness ends in forced labor." Education is not about college or school, but life.

The experience of a pioneer is one who leads by example in doing what is not expected. Being available to accomplish is what I told my sons over and over again, "If you don't try, you have already failed." So, if at first, you don't succeed, try, try again. The simplicity of life is to just let yourself try.

Have you ever seen a spoiled child that has not been disciplined throw a fit and even try to manipulate their parents by holding their breath until they turn blue? Well, if so you let them. When they pass out the body takes control and they start breathing again because of the innate (inborn; natural) application of the system which God put in all of our bodies.

There is no such thing as a square ball. The nature of a ball which is round in all perimeters is made to roll. God created you with purpose, once you start **To Pursue Excellence** the process starts to take effect and you are going places, doing things above average. Developing habits that develop success and make choices that develop successful habits. Making your bed every morning is starting your day with an accomplishment.

In my days of pastoring, we had a standard where the confession of what we wanted had to do with "excellence as a standard, not a byword". But as time went on, we said excellence is tolerated but perfection is required. Quality is the sale of desire. In my book, The Power of Choice, many relevant truths are applied to growth, change, and lasting results.

You are sovereign like God! God created you in His image, and that is inside out, not so much outside as in. No one can make you do anything you do not want to unless you submit or surrender your will. In World War 2 there was a prisoner in the German concentration camp named Victor Frankel. He made a statement after the war was over that was so profound, the Germans could control when I eat, what I eat, where I slept and how I slept. They controlled my outside world, but they could never control what was my inside. They never controlled how I thought or what I thought, only I could do that. **Pursue Excellence!**

Priorities start with preference. There is responsibility and there is accountability, but the fulfillment of one's heart is linked to enjoyment, anticipation, application with acceleration; and then celebration has come into place because of the desired accomplishment. If people would develop habits that can improve their lifestyles, like learning another language, exercising their body and mind, while developing skills that can be beneficial in helping others.

Being a first responder is like the first one to help save a life or do volunteer work to help one's community and country. The great President John F. Kennedy said, "My fellow Americans, ask not what your country can do for you, ask what you can do for your country." **Pursue Excellence!** Having an attitude of servanthood is the compassion of helping others. Matthew 7:12 "Therefore all things whatsoever ye would that men should do to you, do ye even so to them: for this is the law and the prophets."

The one who created you is watching what you do with the abilities he put in you. He makes this statement about Caleb, who was one of the two spies that came back with the good report of taking the land that God gave to them. Ten spies were afraid, but Joshua and Caleb saw potential and they did not take the side of the fearful but were willing to sacrifice to accomplish and obtain.

In Numbers 14:24 it says, "But my servant Caleb, because he had another spirit with him, and hath followed me fully, him will I bring into the land where into he went; and his seed shall possess it." God did not allow the 10 spies that had a negative report go into the promised land. **Pursue Excellence!**

In the book of Genesis 25:22-26 there is the birth of twins, 22"And the children struggled together within her; and she said if it is so, why am I thus? And she went to inquire of the Lord. 23 And the Lord said unto her, two nations are in thy womb, and two types of people shall be separated from thy bowels; and the one people shall be stronger than the other people, and the elder shall serve the younger. 24 And when her days to be delivered were fulfilled, behold, there were twins in her womb. 25 And the first came out red, all over like a hairy garment; and they called his name Esau. 26 And after that came his brother out, and his hand took hold on Esau's heel; and his name was called Jacob." The name Jacob means, "He takes by the heel", or "He deceives."

The reason I want you to see the hidden message God put in the stories of the beginning of the nation of Israel, is that there is a moment in your life which can change your whole life because you have a destiny to fulfill a God-given purpose. In all that Jacob went through to live out what others said about him, God changed his name and future. In this scenario the angel of God changed Jacobs name to Israel, to set a pattern for the birth of excellence.

Genesis 35:16-18 says, 16 "They left Bethel, and when they were still some distance from Ephrath, Rachel went into hard labor. 17 During her difficult labor, the midwife said to her, "Don't be afraid. You have another son." [18] As her life faded away, just before she died, she named him Ben-oni, but his father named him Benjamin.

According to the Hebrew Bible, Benjamin's name was changed deliberately from the name Benoni to Benjamin. This is because Jacob knew that the name, Benoni was descriptive of the pain of Rachel's experienced during her delivery, and its meaning meant, a son of great pain. Jacob knew calling his son by the name Rachel gave would be putting a curse on the child. So, he changed the name to Benjamin in Hebrew which means son of my right hand.

Changing your thinking will change your lifestyle. **Pursue Excellence!** God never waste words, time or power! Everything He does has a purpose. So, you can learn to live by James 2:12-13 [12]So speak ye, and so do, as they that shall be judged by the perfect law of liberty. [13]For he shall have judgment without mercy, that hath shewed no mercy; and mercy rejoices against judgment. See what you sow, is, what you reap. The greatest investment you will ever make is in yourself.

In our book, Reproduction: The Making of a Disciple, the whole picture is about leading by example. I can remember being told by my Dad, "Boy! Do like I say, not as I do!" That is not the example set in motion by

Jesus. In John 5:19-20, [19] Jesus responded to the Jewish leaders, "I assure you that the Son can't do anything by himself except what he sees the Father doing. Whatever the Father does, the Son does likewise. [20] The Father loves the Son and shows him everything that he does. He will show him greater works than these so that you will marvel. Many will walk in your steps as they follow you from a distance. So, **Pursue Excellence!**

In Psalms 119:66, Gods servant says, "Teach me good judgment and knowledge. For I have believed thy commandments." and Psalms 119:99 says, "I have more understanding than my teachers." What you allow in your life affects your life, which is why Proverbs 4:23 states "Keep thy heart with all diligence; for out of it are the real issues of life." So, the seeds of thoughts, attitudes of influence, movies, books, friends, teachers, pastors, and politicians all can put you in the wrong or right path of life. A seed of thought can bring insecurity, rejection and even addictions. So, Guard Your Heart! Mark 4:27 says, "And should sleep, and rise night and day, and the seed should spring and grow up, he knows not how." The sower sows the word, and in you is the ability of God. Mark 4:3-32 is a good read for you.

Desire amplifies ability and discipline increases results.

I can remember in my younger days I worked all night and would listen again and again and again to the word of God being read to me. The majority of my life, I have gone to bed with the word of God being read out loud while I slept. Believe me, it is loud enough for my daughter and whoever is in my house to hear it also. God spoke to Joshua and told him to forget Moses was dead, and to meditate day and night the word of God for him to have the success that God had called him too (Joshua 1:8). In learning the culture of Heaven, one must have one's mind washed by the water of the word (Ephesians 5:26).

So, in my words **Pursue Excellence! Pursue God!** For in Mark 9:23 "Jesus said unto him, if thou canst believe, all things *are* possible to him that can believe."

Choices are not always in our hands but holding on or letting go is!

Chapter Six:

To Your Own Self Be True

Throughout 47 years of ministry at the time of this book's writing, I have had loving, kind, and in their own eyes, considerate people critique and question my personality. I have had people say that I do not preach in love or ask why do you preach like you're mad?

I remember one pastor critiqued me after the Sunday morning service where we had two deaf ears open, and one blind eye healed. Souls were saved and an awesome display of God's power and he said, "no doubt that God uses you, but it sounds like you don't preach in love."

As I was driving home, I was praying and broken in my emotions based on what the pastor had said. Then audibly I heard God speak to me these words: "Mark, not only do I love you, but I like you!" That hit me so hard that I lost it emotionally. I began to weep uncontrollably as I quickly pulled off the road.

Understand what I am saying, you can love anyone or everyone up close or at a distance. But the ones you hang with or enjoy spending time with them, are the ones you like. In some ways liking someone is more personal than love. If you cannot believe in yourself, you will doubt your destiny.

Some of the writings of William Shakespeare speak to me beyond average and amplify the possible. Then when learning the culture of Heaven, and applying the principles and even the commands of Jesus by loving your neighbor as you love yourself (Mark 12:33), choices are not always in our hands but holding on or letting go is!

Raising a young lady during school and reminding her to **Be Responsible,** has everything to do with, **To Thy Own Self Be True!** The plan of waking up at a certain time so we could get ready and not be late for school. Any parent can be in control, but am I raising my children to think like me or think for themselves? Am I raising a child to stay a child or turn into a responsible adult? The aspects of the applications of responsibility are also the consequences of neglect, procrastination or excuses. Laziness has its repercussions, and procrastination has its consequences.

The issue at hand is developing The Power of Choices, and also The Power of Love, which an average individual must be honest with themselves, or pay the piper. This statement comes from an old folklore story about a Pied Piper who was guaranteed a certain amount of money to get rid of an excessive amount of rats in a small township.

But the leaders of the town lied, and did not keep their word, so the Pied Piper blew his flute, and played the musical tune that put all the children under a spell. Then leading them off into another land as he took them far, far, away from their families.

Self-deception is under the spell of indifference, procrastination, excuses, neglect which all falls under the attitude of laziness. Passivity is the attitude of irresponsible individuals no matter the reason, or excuses. When life is taken seriously, consideration of what I do or don't do establishes thought patterns of choice. **To Thy Own Self Be True!**

I am reminded of the old tale I heard as a child. Oooey Gooey was a worm. A mighty worm was he. He climbed upon a railroad track and Oooey Gooey was he. Freedom is what a young man or young lady experience when time has separated them from being a child to being an adult. I have made the statement many times jokingly. If I had known babies turned into teenagers, I would not have had any.

But I say that with a jest or jokingly. I am now experiencing my daughter learning how to drive, and to this day, I am the passenger, and I still tell her what I told her brothers. Get off that white line is a repeated statement, because that is what separates the road from the ditch, or grass, or even an electrical pole.

To develop trust is to develop a love for the truth. So, as we started in the toddler age where communication is established, we kept using the phrase of **Always Tell the Truth!** But the cycle of life is built on two irrefutable issues; knowledge and wisdom. Knowledge comes from books which establishes a foundation, while we are learning wisdom from our personal experiences in life. My kids can ice skate really well, as for me I have to stay close to the wall. Practice, practice, practice is the foundation of experience, especially with music being a part of my life as I was growing up, so I chose to engraft or develop the gifts that I believed was in each of my children.

I wanted to raise each of them individually different, but the same. But I have to admit, the oldest was the experimental child, and the last being my daughter who is the spoiled one, as said by her brothers. But experience brought different applications. **Love is**

Considerate, but it should also be based on: Love your neighbor as you love yourself.

In Galatians 5:20 the Apostle Paul is writing and stated that one of the works of the flesh is witchcraft, and this being in the church. Witchcraft is not always black cats and pointed hats with flying brooms. Jesus said, "If you love me, you will keep my commandments." Luke 10:27 says "And he answered them saying, "Thou shalt love the Lord thy God with all thy heart, and with all thy soul, and with all thy strength, and with all thy mind; and thy neighbor as thyself." As stated, **To Thy Own Self Be True!**

The works of witchcraft manifest in these applications: to intimidate, to manipulate and to control. All witchcraft is working with the intent to seduce, sedate, and ensnare their prey. If Satan can manipulate your emotions, he will manipulate your lifestyle.

One of the greatest weaknesses of Christians many times is insecurity. The unconscious desire to please others or not having a conflict, stims from not knowing the value of one's self-worth or even the fear of being wrong. Insecurity is Satan's strongest weapon in churches. Fear is the opposite of faith and connected to self-preservation.

Confidence is powerful when it is based on trust, love, and peace. One of the greatest scriptures is in Proverbs 3:5 and 6: "Trust in the LORD with all thine heart; and lean not unto thine own understanding. In all your ways acknowledge Him, and he shall direct thy paths." Knowing God's word and knowing who you are in Christ is very important.

The world wants you to believe that what you don't know, will not hurt you. But the lack of knowledge puts you in a disadvantage. The more I know, the less confusion I deal with. Confidence can stand up to a bully. Fear is in the "what if" and "you don't know" imagination realm. God's "people perish for lack of knowledge" is stated in Isaiah 5:13 and Hosea 4:6 says "My people are destroyed for lack of knowledge":

To Thy Own Self Be True! We should always be in agreement and harmony with the Holy Spirit. Doctrines of devils and sensual carnal men are increasing in today's world. Developing one's ability to know the voice of Jesus and the Holy Spirit with confidence is, and should be every believer's priority.

We have compromised truth for the sake of not offending others. The PC (politically correct) doctrine that is running rampant is amazing. The language is traveling in and out of cultures, schools, families, etc., but who wrote the language? Who founded, or created this foreign language known as politically correctness which has taken over lives to live in fear of being branded, and not sure of acceptance?

Confidence is lacking as fear taunts itself as an act of wisdom, when really it is demonic manipulation. See, the devil knows that if he can take away your voice, he can take away your choice, and you become slaves in fear of being branded as phobic, racist, or extremist. When we stand on the truth we will never stand alone. The past, the present, and the future always will expose the truth. The truth will be uncovered no matter how well its hid.

What caused Peter to walk on water was based on what he believed about Jesus. What you believe about Jesus and yourself must be aligned. Galatians 2:20 tells me that I live by the faith of the Son of God, and faith is the substance of what is expected. So, His opinion of you is what you want to live as you manifest his pleasure in your life. As the Prophet Amos said, "How can two walk together without the power of agreement?"

Nothing can be changed or pursued if we live in fear of what others might think. **To Thy Own Self Be True!** My Dad taught me a principle that is really simple. He said God has no green lights, only yellow lights, and red lights. Being a doer of Gods word, automatically allows the Spirit of the Living God to lead us, guild us, He sends us, and even commands us to be doers of the Word of God which is symbolic as are green lights.

In Matthew 28 Jesus said Go ye into all the World! His statement is a green light and for you who have not understood what I am referring to. The green light represents go, the yellow lights refers to caution, and the red light represents stop. In Romans 8:14 it tells us that as many as are led by the spirit of God are the sons of God. If God says no, it is an instant red light. If you are not sure about something, caution is a yellow light.

The ability to be lead by the Holy Spirit is like learning how to drive, this can be a challenge as me teaching my daughter how to drive. I must trust, be patient and not allow anxiety (fear) to be my guild. My daughter's driving will get better and my nerves will too. I will develop confidence and be able to trust her based on experience that has secured my knowledge. Like many things in life change, your confidence should increase above all else. For if you can trust God with your eternity, why can't you trust Him with your today?

There is an old saying of "liar, liar your pants are on fire." Once a liar has been exposed, they been seen uncovered and are no longer able to hide under deception. I am a firm believer in submission to authority, but never submitting to authority beyond my conscience. My conscience is the key of my eternity. So, **To Thy Own Self Be True!**

The Holy Spirit said through Paul in II Thessalonians 2:10,11,12, that many would-be deceived, because they loved not the truth. Deception is the misleading of truth. The chance of a lie being fulfilled, is like the chance of the truth never being fulfilled. A half-truth is a whole lie. God cannot lie, Jesus is the spotless lamb who is the way, the truth, and the life, while the Holy Ghost is the Spirit of Truth.

If you do not know the shepherd's voice, you are in a paradigm shift of a choice. The comparison of others can be the pivotal point of shift that can be the beginning of the misleading of the truth. Many will be deceived because it is what they want to believe, as Paul said "heaping unto themselves teachers that scratch itching ears," as stated in II Timothy 4:3: **To Thy Own Self Be True!**

When Jesus called Satan the father of lies in John 8:44, it is because Satan gave birth to a lie when he believed he could ascend to the most high and be like God. There is no truth in a lie, other than it's a lie; for a little leaven leavens the whole lump. "Except the Lord build the house those that labor; labor in vain" as stated in Psalms 127:1. When the river of life really begins to flow, so shall the sovereignty of God, and we will see and know as never before. Our days are numbered not in defeat, but in the display of God's people taking their seat in the authority of who He is.

The light will increase in the midst of the wars that seem not to cease. **To Thy Own Self Be True!** We are called to be a triumphant Church, a triumphant people. The heavier the anointing the greater responsibility and principles of establishing a natural foundational trust in yourself, God's word, and the Holy Spirit that lives in and with every born-again believer.

But, remember that witchcraft is manipulation, intimidation, and control. Knowing that this is not just demons, but the sinful nature still has place in churches. Never and I mean never be controlled by other people's money, people status, or their titles, or past experiences. Submission to authority should never mean letting someone control your conscience. You alone are responsible for your choices. The blame game is not strong enough to stand on. Jesus is your rock, all others are sinking sand. **To Thy Own Self Be True!**

The emotions of one's flesh or feelings can summon up false realities that can cause the blind to lead the blind, and those that fall into the ditch will find it difficult to get back into the straight and narrow path of righteousness. The leaven of the Pharisees was deception to keep misleading the people with partial truth so that the leaders did not have to be accountable for their lies.

The Holiness of God will purge out the pulpit of many. For the Chief Shepherd will not allow the under-shepherds to keep leading His sheep astray. John 15 stated that we need the purging and pruning to take place as stated in I Peter 4:7, "But the end of all things is at hand: be ye therefore sober and watch unto prayer." **To Thy Own Self Be True!"**

The pruning and purging will begin in the leadership of the body of Christ, and as the presence of God does increase, manifestations of signs and wonders will be released as visible encounters with angels will begin and not cease. The war in the heavenlies is over the truth, not control over the earth, because God is alpha and omega. Winston Churchill said, **"Fear is a reaction, but Courage is a decision."**

How would you like to compromise your eternity? Then what are you doing with your moment? We can create our future, or we can recreate our past. Priorities start with preference. There is responsibility and there is accountability, but the fulfillment of one's heart is linked to enjoyment, anticipation, application with acceleration; because celebration has come into place because of desired accomplishment. **To Thy Own Self Be True!**

I am firm to believe we can go beyond where we have been led. I love the phrase on an old television show called Star Trek that was on during 1966 till 1999, "Going where no man has gone before." Believing beyond the imagination of others, created a computer that can fit in your hand that has more power than the computer that put man on the moon. It's called a cell phone. If we took the cell phone of today and went back in time, we would be considered aliens.

I am amazed by the intelligence that continues to go where no man has gone before. What alarms me is the computer chip the size of a grain of rice. The size is small and if a grain of mustard seed faith can be great, so even the more a computer chip the size of a grain of rice can destroy your eternity. For no matter who you are if you take the mark of the beast, there is no redemption for you. It is possible this chip is the mark of the beast. The hard part in life is overcoming the influence of our past, overcoming this is alone needed to free up the flow of our future. Have faith in God to warn you, to lead you and direct your path in life.

As Paul said in Philippians 3:13 "Brethren, I count not myself to have apprehended: but this one thing I do, forgetting those things which are behind, and reaching forth unto those things which are before," The Holy Spirit told me, "What you take for granted can be taken from you." Take not eternity lightly.

In Shakespeare's, Hamlet, Act 1, scene 3, 78–82, we find that Polonius: spoke to his son this phrase. "This above all: to thine own self be true, and it must follow, as the night the day, Thou canst not then be false to any man." "To thine own self be true" is Polonius's last piece of advice to his son Laertes, who is in a hurry to get on the next boat to Paris, where he'll be safe from his father's long-winded speeches.

We can run from life in many directions but, **To Thy Own Self Be True!** If you stay true to yourself, you'll never have regrets. What you do in secret will eventually surface in public. Never put limits on the truth for what you believe in. For what you believe in, you invest in. So, believe in yourself, no matter what others might say, believe in yourself.

In relationships we have three different types of friends. Close, Casual, and Intimate. Close you choose, Casual the other party chooses, and Intimate is a gift from God. Usually, there is only a few which have lifelong friends which they can trust and know no matter what they will be there for you. **To Thy Own Self Be True!** Everybody has or will have a Judas in their lives. Someone that will let you down that you have put trust in. But know this that what Galatians 6:7 says is worth its weight in gold. "God is not mocked or taken lightly.

God is not history, but the creator of the past, present, and the future. You sow or plant corruption your will reap corruption, but if you give life you will receive a harvest of loving life. So, **Always Tell the Truth**, know that **Love is Considerate, Be Responsible, Have Integrity, Pursue Excellence, To Your Own Self Be True** and **Control Your Attitude** while **Being Safe is Wisdom**.

In traveling through a looking glass, I was surprised by what one could see. The reflections of what I thought was truly someone else and really not me. For tho my past was visible, the moments seem clearly a different type of what should be. My destiny is before me as my choices create change or should I just let it be.

Dr. Mark D. White

Don't walk past your future, because of the stubbornness of your past.

Chapter Seven:
Control Your Attitude

Keeping one's attitude in check is a serious issue in life. It is like the temperature in the room, everyone is uncomfortable, or comfortable with your influence at the moment. Your attitude brands you of what others will expect out of you. All it takes is just based on what they saw for a moment. **Your attitude is the display of your faith and expectancy in yourself and others.** There are scientific classifications of personalities, like the extrovert and introvert. What others may think of you is not as important as what you think of you. Jesus said to love your neighbor as much as you love yourself in Mark 12:30-31:

> 30 "and thou shalt love the Lord thy God with all thy heart, and with all thy soul, and with all thine understanding, and with all thy strength. This is the first commandment. 31 "And a second like it is this: Thou shalt love thy neighbor as thyself. There is not another commandment greater than these."

Introvert comes from Latin intro-, "inward," and vertere, "turning." It describes a person who tends to turn inward mentally, sometimes avoiding large groups of people. Introverts tend to be a type B personality, which are not driven to be in control. The opposite of an introvert is an extrovert, who finds energy in interactions with others, while having a natural expression of how they feel and see things. Extroverts tend to be type A and some type B personalities, and also natural leaders.

A person's attitude is a subjected inward response to their feelings, and their response to situations, or circumstances that they approve or disapprove of. An attitude is like your face, and actions are like a map of where you come from, and where you are going. No matter how science sees you in classification, you are a representation of a certain definitive purpose.

God created you with purpose and it is up to you to utilize and develop you gifts and calling. I have found it strange that people who are the quite ones are the one to watch. The extrovert expresses what they think, but the introvert keeps you wondering. So, **Control Your Attitude** if you want to lead and make a difference.

The old folklore about a frog in the kettle is descriptive of the gradual submitting to your circumstances. If you put a frog in hot water it will hop out, but if you put the frog in cold water which is being gradually heated, the frog submits, and is gradually overcome by its circumstances. This is the same trap Satan sets for you, he seduces you, he sedates you, then ensnares you.

Having an opinion should begin in your spirits consciousness of God's Word, and what is the Holy Spirit saying, or is He giving you a cautious sense to take notice of your surroundings? Without knowing, we at times have allowed the enemy to have the upper hand, or the advantage on us. This by being with the wrong people at the wrong time seduces you to accept what others are doing, then sedates you where it's ok to be part of the crowd, and this opens the trap of being ensnared and manipulated.

Control Your Attitude! As a little boy, I was very conscious of the presence and power of God. My mother told me that during my earlier days around 4 years old, 'till about 8 years old, I would play with the neighborhood kids and have disagreements that brought me to a place of hurt and frustration.

My mother told me that I would come into the house stomping my boots, and I would stick out my pouting lips. Then I would put on an LP record of Evangelist Jimmy Swaggart singing and playing the piano. I would play both sides of the record, and then go outside to play again. This happened sometimes two or three times a day.

The anointing makes a difference in one's attitude. It "destroys the yoke" is what Isaiah 10:27 tells us. Adults or teenagers should never have unforgiveness in their lives. We are to be influenced by the Holy Spirit, and the word of God, not by feelings. Attitudes are somewhat a response to feelings, or influence from situations, or individuals.

Romans 6:16 tells us of who or what we submit to is what determines our lives. Righteousness or unrighteousness, right or wrong, good or evil. Your attitude displays who you submit to. If Satan can manipulate your emotions, he will manipulate your lifestyle. So, **Control Your Attitude!** Don't be the frog in the kettle, don't pout when you don't get your way. Worship is the key to the miraculous.

In my years of pastoring, I had a standard, based on choice. In life, everybody has a bad day where something or someone offended us, or life seems hopeless. I have always used the analogy that God plays baseball. Strike one is grace, strike two is mercy and strike three is judgment. A bad attitude is yielding to a wrong influence, bad situations or situational hopelessness.

As long as there is repentance or there is an attitude change, there is forgiveness. That is strike one. But when a negative attitude is continued for two weeks and not adjusted, or an effort made to confront the problem, that is strike two, which is mercy. But, when week three still displays a bad negative attitude, we need to talk, or the person needs to walk. The attitude changes, or you're not needed in leadership. See a leader leads by example. So, **Control Your Attitude!**

You might have influenced people as a peacemaker and you are an introvert, even more now, you are needed as an extrovert. To make peace, you must be strong in war as a nation, a church, a family, or an individual. For if you do not defeat the enemy in the spirit realm, he will try to control you in the natural realm. If the Devil can manipulate your emotions, he will manipulate your lifestyle.

We wrestle not against flesh and blood, but against principalities and powers of darkness (Ephesians 6:12). The one thing is, God sees what you don't do in being a Christian and God sees as much as what you do. Controlling your Attitude is strategic as much as investing. An action or reaction is like a seed which will impact and produce a harvest. For what you do in secret will be brought forth to be seen. So to be at peace with yourself, having a prayer life and consistent relationship with Jesus and Holy Spirit make a world of difference. **Control Your Attitude!**

A silent smile with a peaceful and confident facial expression will create a standard of resistance of being intimidated or controlled. In school we learned that it is the silent one that is unpredictable. The very vocal was usually the insecure flaunting themselves as if they knew everything.

Confidence and Peace are like twins, separated at birth, but totally alike in character and purpose. Just because you seem to lack ability does not me you lack peace or confidence. Evaluation of a situation or circumstance allows an action to be taken without thought to help or prevent a situation.

One of my favorite scriptures is Psalms 119:165: "Great peace have they which love thy law: and nothing shall offend them." And also, I really like to live by and highly recommend Isaiah 26:3: "Thou wilt keep *him* in perfect peace, *whose* mind *is* stayed *on thee*: because he trusts in thee." What you favor is what you are drawn to.

What you desire is what you seek for. What is your nature, is your lifestyle. Develop the ability of being a "new creation" as stated in 2nd Corinthians 5:17. A professional person in the business field of life works at how they represent the company they work for, and how others think about them is a lasting effect. To be your best is not a façade, but it is developed by association and impartation.

Once you reach a place of confidence, you project what you have peace in, and display what is your comfort zone. **Control Your Attitude**, develop it. You will maintain control of how you respond in public and private. You are an overcomer by the blood of the Lamb and the words of your mouth (Revelations 12:11).

Faith is an attitude and fear tries to manipulate one's attitude. It is not always publicly expressed but through it, the seed of thought take root. They begin to express expectancy. Fear and Faith have the ability to create something out of nothing, and bring into existence that which does not exist.

The repetition of saying the same thing over and over again or as some call it meditation, pondering, or envisioning. It's like the elderly woman that said to herself in Matthew 9:21, "For she said within herself, If I may but touch his garment, I shall be whole." She envisioned, she set in motion what she wanted by thinking and applying herself to reach out and touch Jesus. To receive what she believed she could get by just touching his garment was an act of faith which was an Attitude.

She controlled her attitude, based on what she wanted, and not on what others thought. By the culture of her people she could have been stoned to death. By law she had to stay away from people and cry out the statement of "unclean, unclean." Your response in life should always be bigger than other people's problem. Never let others steal your joy, hope or endurance. **Control Your Attitude**.

You are not a puppet manipulated by circumstances. The book of Daniel says the righteous are as bold as a lion. Confidence is peace, patience, and faith all based on love. Patience is the strength of your tomorrow. Patience is the hope of your future, the dream of your desires. For without Patience, you have no Peace. It is with faith and patience that we obtain the promise. (Hebrews 6:12) Patience is not just a frame of mind, but an attitude maintained over time.

A person of faith is not someone who is stubborn or foolish, but someone full of peace and confidence that allows patience to rule. There is something called the process of elimination, which is a filtering of what you accept and what you reject. This is the power of choice. Feelings can influence your response, but the power of choice can suppress and control them instead of them controlling you. If you can trust God with your eternity, why can't you trust him with your today?

Here is the definition of the word attitude: a settled way of thinking or feeling about someone or something, typically one that is reflected in a person's behavior. In controlling your thoughts, this has everything to do with your response, in your actions, or even a long-term response. Proverbs 4:23 says "Guard your heart with all that is in you, for out of it comes the issues of life."

You are not a puppet where someone can pull your strings to manipulate your response, which can be your attitude. **Control Your Attitude!** See if you don't try, you have already failed. A smile is the beginning of laughter. Go to the mirror and smile, because the door is now open to laugh at situations because you see the hope in you needed to win.

Desire amplifies ability and discipline increases results.

When life seems hopeless, you feed your hope. When answers are fleeting, you keep asking questions. When fear is overwhelming you embrace peace, and refuse to give in, or surrender to things and situations. Everything in life is set to give an opportunity to those that fight to have faith in God's faithfulness. Receiving a miracle, and receiving an answer to prayers is all about rebelling against your circumstances while standing on Gods promises and speaking His word.

Your attitude is your confidence, your peace and your faith in action as you respond in life situations.

We are light in darkness, not in the dark with no light. Jesus is our answer, He cannot lie, His promises are yes and amen. We are overcomers by the Blood of the Lamb and the words of our mouth. Again, I say If you can trust God with your eternity, why can't you trust him with your today? **Control Your Attitude!**

The Apostle Paul said in Romans 8:31: "If God be for us, who can be against us!" Then in verses 37-39 and then Romans 9:1.

> 37Nay, in all these things we are more than conquerors through him that loved us. 38For I am persuaded, that neither death, nor life, nor angels, nor principalities, nor powers, nor things present, nor things to come, 39Nor height, nor depth, nor any other creature, shall be able to separate us from the love of God, which is in Christ Jesus our Lord. Romans 9:1: "I say the truth in Christ, I lie not, my conscience also bearing me witness in the Holy Ghost,"

There are associated inclinations of different people, who see things defiantly based on their temperament or personality. There is a proto-psychological theory which suggests that there are four distinct fundamental personality types, called sanguine, choleric, melancholic, and phlegmatic. Most interpretations of these include the possibility of mixtures between the types where an individual's personality types overlap, and they share two or more temperaments.

I can see a mixture of a couple of these types working in my life. I have even been accused of having Attention Deficit Hyperactivity Disorder (ADHD) by a loving caring family member. It really does not matter to me anymore. I enjoy having my thoughts bouncing around in my head like a ping pong ball. Jokingly I could say God has ADHD, He is multi-tasking all the time.

No matter what others say, you still can **Control Your Attitude!** Keeping your mouth closed, and not expressing yourself immediately can make a difference. Making the choice to smile and not turn extravert expressive in a display of your thoughts. Keeping your mouth closed is the beginning of controlling your thoughts. Philippians 4:8 gives a direction of thought categories to ponder. "Finally, brethren, whatsoever things are true, whatsoever things are honest, whatsoever things are just, whatsoever things are pure, whatsoever things are lovely, whatsoever things are of good report; if there be any virtue, and if there be any praise, think on these things." Thoughts create actions:

Be careful of your thoughts, for your thoughts become your words. Be careful of your words, for your words become your actions. Be careful of your actions, for your actions become your habits. Be careful of your habits for your habits become your character. Be careful of your character, for your character creates your future. (author unknown)

There are many who are controlled by a deceiving spirit called apathy which is also known as being lukewarm or passive. Some want to think that God is in control and they don't have to do anything. But in Luke 10:19 Jesus said that He has given us authority. The plight of God your creator, is if He cannot get you to fast, and pray, to cry aloud, to sound the alarm, to seek His face, to pull down strongholds. If you are not willing to seek the face of Jesus, then what can be done to give you victory?

If you are Anti-Bible, you are being controlled by the Anti-Christ spirit. These are the last days as you will know by the signs of the times. You will either fight, do what's right or take flight. Realize that God sees what you're not doing as much as He sees what is being done! "So, blessed are the peacemakers, for they shall be called the children of God," (Matthew 5:9).

The ones who have a prayer life can pray instantly in private or in public. Passion is an attitude and Jesus said in Matthew 5:6, "Blessed are those that hunger and thirst after righteousness: for they shall be filled." If you are hungry for more of God, your attitude is different than those that are indifferent.

You have to quit being a closet Christian, for if you do not have a voice, you will lose your choice, in being a light unto the world, and unto your generation. So, what can you do to represent your faith in God faithfulness? It is up to your choice to pursue doing as Jesus did in living for others salvation. Taking up your cross to follow Jesus, His Word, and the Holy Spirit is an awesome experience. **Control Your Attitude!**

Be as Romans 12:1-2 says: "I beseech you therefore, brethren, by the mercies of God, that ye present your bodies a living sacrifice, holy, acceptable unto God, *which is* your reasonable service." 2"And be not conformed to this world: but be ye transformed by the renewing of your mind, that ye may prove what *is* that good, and acceptable, and perfect, will of God."

You can recreate your past by doing nothing or you can work to create a future by investing in growing up in Christ. **Control Your Attitude!** As a Dad, I remind myself and my children, it's my responsibility to guard and guild. No matter how people respond or think. I am responsible to love like Jesus. No greater love has anyone than to lay down their life for their friend.

Words can be short, but the meaning
long. Life is like the weather the changes
continue on. My fortitude is beyond logic
because it's dependent on God's Grace
and without His Mercy, some things
would not take place. The battle may be
the Lords, but the responsibility of victory
is mine. In the midst of each battle, my
attitude is what should shine. At times
there is remorse for what I want things to
be, having just one word in due season
defies the logic of what I cannot see!

Dr. Mark D. White

Proverbs 4:23 "Keep thy heart with all diligence; for out of it are the issues of life."

Chapter Eight:

Being Safe is Wisdom

Saying to my daughter these phrases, again and again, is not just being repetitive, but this builds one's confidence. In 2 Timothy 1:7, Apostle Paul says "For God hath not given us the spirit of fear; but the spirit of power, and the spirit of love, and the spirit of a sound mind." As the world turns so does life deal with changes that can affect someone for the rest of their life.

The aspect of being safe is not taking things for granted, not totally trusting people blindly. Thinking for yourself is a step of being safe. True the system is set up for humanity to be co-dependent. But, again and again I remind her of that privilege has a responsibility, and trusting the Holy Spirit to the knowing of His voice is being safe while listening for wisdom.

God has given His people the right to cast out devils, but not all evil is demonic activity or witchcraft. Some things are done because of corruption in people with evil hearts. Having the right attitude is easier when there is confidence not only in God, but also in His Word and even angels. Having confidence is wisdom applied toward the scripture of "Giving no place to the Devil," as stated in Ephesians 4:27, is wisdom! **"Being Safe is Wisdom."**

There are mental battles, physical battles, and even financial battles. But spiritual warfare is not the cause of all activity in some people. Thieves are not always demon-possessed, or bullies or individuals with anger issues are not always demon-possessed. I can bind devils with the name of Jesus, but I cannot bind people. One of the scriptures that can make a difference in one's life is in 2 Corinthians 6:14, "Be ye not unequally yoked together with unbelievers: for what fellowship hath righteousness with unrighteousness? and what communion hath light with darkness?" **"Being Safe is Wisdom."**

Where you live and, the laws and cultures of your nation, or your personal view may not agree with some of the things I say, but I can live with that. One of my many statements is, "love protects what it loves." Even doing typical work, I remember when I was young, I was an electrician's apprentice, and I remember one thing that has stayed with me for years. Safety at any price is worth the price. To **Be Responsible** is to realize that what happens to you affects others. Life can be dangerous. Use Wisdom!

One of the churches I pastored I was in the attic doing some electrical work. The wiring was showing 110 but it was wired with two breakers that made it 220 and I did not know that. What I took for granted almost took my life. The guy I was working with told me the breaker was off, but we did not know it was wired for 220 using two 110's breakers. So, I got shocked while I was shouting, "Turning it off," believe me, I was shaken to the bone. Thank God I am still alive. I want you to see, what you take for granted can be taken from you. **"Being Safe is Wisdom."**

My Dad was a Marine Drill Sergeant, and he taught my brothers and I some strong rules and understanding. One that I remember was that He said "if you start a fight, he would whip me, if you run from a fight, he would whip me." "He said it does not matter who wins or loses as much as the other person knowing that you had been there."

Defending yourself is just as important as how you walk away. Running to a battle is standing up internally, before you express yourself externally. Anger is not the right attitude in dealing with problems or problem people. Apostle Paul said in Ephesians 4:26 "To not let the sun go down on your anger." Controlling how you think is the power of controlling how you act. It is to your advantage to **Control Your Attitude**, because for you to apply Wisdom in Being Safe, confidence makes the difference, and peace feeds your patience. Confidence is the display of peace.

The Bible gives warfare and battle armor as symbolic structures to build an understanding we are at war. This is not to be taken casually, but serious and life threating. The armor mentioned in Ephesians 6:10-19 shows us about the sword of the spirit and the shield of faith, the helmet of salvation, etc... But being safe is like walking down the street in town at night. The sidewalk is made for the day, but the middle of the road is safer at night, unless traffic is an issue. Why? Evil hides in darkness to surprise you, to try to overtake you.

But, not being immediately accessible is wisdom, so depending on the situation, the middle is better than left or right. I have worked the streets in the French Quarters in New Orleans, sharing Jesus working in a Christian coffee house as I witnessed to gays and prostitutes. I remember being warned that the girls coming out of certain nightclub was transvestites. But wow, did the guys ever look like beautiful looking women, it was amazing. As the old saying goes, a possum ran over my grave, this is an old country saying describing you just had chill bumps run all over you. So, **"Being Safe is Wisdom."**

I remember a Jesus march I was a part of during Mardi Gras in New Orleans in the French Quarters. In French, the word "Mardi" means "Tuesday," and the word "gras" means "fat," meaning that Mardi Gras translates to English as "Fat Tuesday.". The name comes from the practice of preparing for the start of a period of fasting on Ash Wednesday, which immediately follows Mardi Gras. Mardi Gras is the Catholic Christian festival of Shrove Tuesday, the day before Lent, which people in some places celebrate by wearing colorful costumes and dancing through the streets.

The Mardi Gras is a celebration which is a time of drunken perversion in parties and parades. I was separated from the group I was working with. This march was called a silent Jesus march as it was to display banners, signs with the Gospel of Jesus while not saying a word. This Jesus march had over two hundred Christians walking in a line carrying banners of God love and what Jesus did to save the world.

How, I somehow got at the end of the line, I do not know. Beer was being thrown at me, cigarettes were flicked at me, being cursed, and spit at as glasses of wine were throw also, but wisdom said, "Stay with the group." There were a lot of drunks fighting during this time of celebrating Madi Gras, while so many people dressed up in different types of costumes. There was this one guy dressed up like a cotton ball 'till someone lit a match. The news reported of how a man had to be rushed to the hospital.

My experiences in my travels remind me, that I need to keep learning, and learning, and learning. **"Being Safe is Wisdom."** I find myself in awe of God's hand of safety that has been there for me, time and time again. I was in Paris, France years ago, and I was staying in the home of a couple that my connections had set for me to stay with.

The night was sleepless, and the warfare was intense. Lots of witchcraft was working against me and the meetings. I was leaving to go wait on my ride to go to a meeting and the person with whom I was staying with blocked the door with his hands, and told me that I was not going to my meeting, that he had called and canceled transportation from picking me up. Repeatedly he kept telling me "You no go" You stay here," he was from Congo and spoke very little English and I spoke no French.

Now that did not set well with me, so I went back to the room and packed my suitcases and begin to walk toward the door to leave. He stood and blocked the door again, and would not let me pass. I told Jesus quietly that if this person would not move from blocking the door, I would have to take necessary action to find my freedom to go preach. I really did not want to show some love with my fist, having named it Mark's chapter five. But God moved him out of my way, and I went out to the streets of Paris, not knowing where I was at in this big city in a foreign country, and my cell phone was not working. I begin to pray. My actions were not logical, but very much relational with the God of all creation.

Father in Jesus name, you know where I am at, and you called me to come here, so I know you have a plan and you will take care of me. I waited for about 20 minutes, and then a white van passed me and they stopped, then backed up, and asked me "are you, Mark White," and I said "Yes." They asked me what are you doing here? I told them, and they picked me up and put me in a hotel. Know the Spirit of Wisdom, build a relationship with the Holy Spirit. Never offend him and always work to please him.

God moved on my behalf, because I believe in His faithfulness, even when I am seemingly faithless. 1 John 5:14,15 says: "And this is the confidence that we have in him, that, if we ask any thing according to his will, he heareth us: And if we know that he hears us: And whatsoever we ask, we know that we have the petitions that we desired of him." God works miracles still today. Mark 9:23 says "If you can believe, all things are possible." Wisdom is experience's reward, books can never teach you wisdom, but knowledge is learning from others understanding for one to apply. **"Being Safe is Wisdom."**

When we are young, we sometimes do things that are dumb. I was squirrel hunting with a friend, and saw up in the top of a tree, a hornets' nest. These nests are like a round oblong paper home for hornets, and hornets are such dangerous bugs that their stings can put you in the hospital. I left my shotgun leaning against the tree, and went back to the house to get an ax. I chopped the tree down, and waited till the swarm of hornets calmed down. My friend and I took a handkerchief and plugged the hole closed with just a stick, a handkerchief and bold, stupid actions. After we cut the limb off from the tree, we marched back to the house like a proud peacock.

I put the nest in the trunk of my car and went home. After a of couple days I was so proud of my trophy that I took it to where I worked, and showed it to my boss. I shook the nest and said "Listen, you can still hear them." He ordered me out of the building. He said, "They made one hole, they can make another one to get out." Innocence can have its reward of stupidity.

God's grace can cover our mistakes, but our accountability is still subject to the law of sowing and reaping, as stated in Galatians 6:7-9: "Let him that is taught in the word communicate unto him that teaches in all good things. 7 Be not deceived; God is not mocked: for whatsoever a man soweth, that shall he also reap. 8 For he that soweth to his flesh shall of the flesh reap corruption; but he that soweth to the Spirit shall of the Spirit reap life everlasting. 9 And let us not be weary in well doing: for in due season we shall reap, if we faint not." Prophet Forrest Gump says, "Stupid is as Stupid does." Having childlike faith does not allow for childlike actions. **"Being Safe is Wisdom."**

There is a statement in Ephesians 4 about equipping the saints. For years I have insisted that my daughter take self-defense lessons. Being prepared is not being negative, but confidence is self-trust, self-knowledge and subconscious knowledge. The roots of a tree go deep in their foundation to tap into a flow of life-giving water. I believe in conceal and carry, and giving no place to the devil. The Apostle Paul said in 2 Corinthians 2:11, "Let not Satan get an advantage of us: be not ignorant of his devices." So, safety at any cost is worth the price. Experience, and repetition build confidence, and as life is not always fair, your judgments or decisions should be weighed in the balance of counsel and experience. **"Being Safe is Wisdom."**

We must protect what God has given us, by not expecting the worst, but being prepared. It's like having a flashlight in case the lights go out. I find myself even when texting my daughter when she is with friends, I say **Be Safe!** Friends can be an asset and a liability. The same things that one would require out of themselves they also should require out of the company of friends they keep. "Corrupt communication corrupts good standards (1 Corinthians 15:33)."

Years ago, the Spirit of God told me that "If one lives off excuses, they can die because of the reasons." If you feed your fear, it grows like weeds and they choke the life out of hope and faith. Having faith in God is not to do nothing, but when you have done all, you stand, and all is doing everything you can. As Ephesians 6:13 says, you must help God help you. **Being Safe is Wisdom!**

Knowing God's word is not enough, you must believe it. Acts 17:28 says "In Him we live and move, and have our very being." Life is too short to not extend your efforts to learn, apply and experience. As James 1:22 says "But be ye doers of the word, and not just hearers only." In the book of Jude verse 22, the Apostle tells you to pray in the Holy Ghost, for in this you build up your most holy faith.

There are only three ways of praying in the Spirit of God. #1 is praying the word of God, #2 is praying in tongues (the Holy Ghost) and #3 is praying as Paul wrote in Romans 8:26-27: praying in the spirit and groanings. Proverbs 4:7 says "Wisdom is the principal thing; therefore, get wisdom: and with all thy getting get understanding."

**If you cannot believe in yourself,
you will doubt your destiny!**

Chapter Nine:
You Are Never Defeated

In the Old Testament, Micah the prophet of God makes this statement; "Rejoice not against me O' my enemy, when I fall, I shall get up." In many different situations, I have spoken this phrase into the lives of my children. "If you don't try, you have already failed"! I love the translation of this verse from the Passion Bible.

> Proverbs 24:16 says "For the lovers of God may suffer adversity and stumble seven times, but they will continue to rise over and over again. But the unrighteous are brought down by just one calamity and will never be able to rise again."

Life can be difficult many times like hills and valleys. The flat plateau can be on the mountain top or in the valley below. Life is the power of choice, and you can overcome it, or it can overcome you. Psalms 107:2 says "Let the redeemed of the Lord say so, whom He has redeemed from the hand of the enemy." The power of influence is many times represented by someone's hand being upon them. That influence can be a touch, a little nudge or the pressure of intimidation. Self Confidence is the power of trusting yourself, and being at peace with one's self in decisions made.

> Psalms 34:19 "Many are the afflictions of the righteous: but the LORD delivers him out of them all."

Those that walk with God are ready to run for Him. The lives of those that live in a higher realm of the spirit are pioneers, also known as forerunners, they go and do what others will follow in. Living by faith is not living by a doctrine but a relationship of trust. When you know in your knower is the old phrase; I can do this!

> Proverbs 3:5-6 tells us "To Trust in the LORD with all thine heart, and lean not unto thine own understanding. 6 In all thy ways acknowledge him, and he shall direct thy paths."

If you cannot see beyond where you are at, you are possibly going to trip over what you do not see. Meaning if you cannot see by faith and trust in God, you will be tempted to quit or you may think you have failed, and you may feel despair and sadness with the temptation to give up. But You will Never Quit!

If you can trust God with your eternity, why can't you trust Him with your today?

The times of failure can create what is also called emotional fatigue. This can even make it seem like the bottom is dropping out. This can have an adverse effect on one's emotions and mental stability. Sadness or prolonged sorrow can turn into a pity party or even depression. The power of choice has to rise to make the committed effort of no matter the pain, the shame or emotional drain, I will not be defeated and I will not quit. You have the ability to pull yourself out of the pit of circumstances. To even climb higher than you are, while setting yourself to seeing beyond your moment. All because the greater one is in you (1 John 4:4) and you can do all things through Christ (Philippians 4:13).

Years ago, the Holy Spirit told me that "If Satan can manipulate your emotions, He will manipulate my lifestyle." Living by faith can be taken into the arena of risk management. Trusting the unseen and believing beyond logic is the aspect of learning the spirit realm and its functions. This is learning as you go, walking where your average individual does not live or even consider. The statement of going where no man has gone before is the application of overcoming our knowledge or lack of knowledge. The culture we were raised in or even one's gender affects our response in standing one's ground to win in life. **"Your limits are your imagination."**

The ways of heaven can only be learned, by learning the language of heaven. In Psalms 103:7 the prophet is giving insight into the deep things of God, "He made known his ways unto Moses, his acts unto the children of Israel." Leaning the voice of the Shepherd and developing the sensitivity of the unction of the Holy Spirit is learning the ways of God. Understanding the actions and communication of angels is learning the ways of heaven.

The language of heaven goes beyond tongues, it is speaking in the total creation of all that God created. From the bees flight to the flying of hummingbirds. To the whisper of the wind to the sound of lightning is now telling you thunder is about to happen. To the rumbling of a small earthquake to the spinning of a tornado which usually spins counterclockwise, but it can spin clockwise as well, though such cases are rare. This is such a display of prophetic language to take your blessings from your past and destroy them, meaning counterclockwise is going back in time.

Jesus is the spirit of prophecy is stated in Revelations 19:10 and prophecy is to declare something before it happens. So also, as stated in Colossians 1:16-17 that by him and in him all things exist. Like the burning bush to Moses, the conversation was started when Moses saw the bush burning before God spoke to Moses in the common language. Revelations 12:11 says "we are overcomers by the blood of the Lamb and the word of our testimony." Just as important to remind you or your place of access is Hebrews 4:16 of "Let us come boldly before the throne of grace that we may receive mercy to help in time of need."

God speaks in our lives to prevent, prepare, to invest, to establish and to accomplish. You are called to represent the creator and that is not a failure. Being like your creator is knowing that your words can change thoughts, actions, and results. In the beginning, when God started with creation it everything was good, except for the part it is not good to be alone. Success is to be shared. **You have no limits unless you restrain yourself!**

You should be listening for what you are not hearing. God is always speaking, teaching, and sharing his ways and purpose. As stated in

> Isaiah 55:6 "Seek ye the LORD while he may be found, call ye upon him while he is near: 7Let the wicked forsake his way, and the unrighteous man his thoughts: and let him return unto the LORD, and

he will have mercy upon him; and to our God, for he will abundantly pardon. 8For my thoughts are not your thoughts, neither are your ways my ways, saith the LORD. 9For as the heavens are higher than the earth, so are my ways higher than your ways, and my thoughts than your thoughts. 10For as the rain comes down, and the snow from heaven, and returns not thither, but waters the earth, and makes it bring forth and bud, that it may give seed to the sower, and bread to the eater: 11So shall my word be that goes forth out of my mouth: it shall not return unto me void, but it shall accomplish that which I please, and it shall prosper in the thing whereto I sent it. 12For ye shall go out with joy, and be led forth with peace: the mountains and the hills shall break forth before you into singing, and all the trees of the field shall clap their hands."

The foundational roots of your natural heritage are worth looking at again and again. The teachings of experiences and the knowledge, which is given by those that love you, and want your best for you, should never exceed the working of God's influence in your life. No matter what the Devil meant for your hurt, will work for your good if you allow the Holy Spirit to seize the day, and give you hope for tomorrow.

When we fail, fall or even quit, the call of Gods plan for your life can never be lifted. No matter what you have experienced in life's painful and frustrating moments, you still will be accountable to do his will for His results, you must pursue your destiny. In our moments of failure or if we fall in some way, you can get up and you can start over.

No one is perfect, but we all are being perfected. Even Jesus learned obedience by the things he suffered as stated in Hebrews 5:8. Your tomorrow is your today, and your today shapes your tomorrow. So choose what you are going to do. Are you going to be like the world or stand on the foundational roots that have been planted inside your sub-conscience? The depth of who you are is in your hands to be that person God called or allow the storms of life to become a tornado and do a counterclockwise move to destroy all that you have invested in. In a moment, one can destroy what took years to build.

You can be an overcomer as stated in Revelations 12:11, by the blood of the Lamb, and the words of your mouth. Your attitude is a language, and you need to make it speak what you want, not what others think. In Philippians 3:13 Apostle Paul directs one to focus on destiny versus memories. So, let us listen to what God speaks clearly about overcoming and getting back up to start over as we break down Philippians 3:13-15.

Forgetting of what is in your past is a major issue. Forgiveness of others and above all forgiveness of oneself are decisions that affect your daily life and eternity (Mark 11:25,26). The influence of what should have been forgiven and forgotten is one of the greatest weapons the enemy can use against you, called condemnation.

The past can so much affect your ability to step in faith it is amazing how a memory can stop one from accomplishing one's heart greatest desires. Faith and fear are two powerful forces. They both have the ability to create something out of nothing and bring into existence what does not exist.

Pressing toward the mark is the beginning of fulfillment into one's destiny. Destiny is a reflection of desire; without a desire, it is difficult to acquire. To pursue is to do. The step of faith may seem difficult, but trust is the invisible force to assist in accomplishment and fulfillment. Your pressing toward the mark is a choice of commitment, discipline, and pursuit.

To walk a thousand miles starts with one step at a time.

Perfect minded is a choice that has to be pursued. When the scripture tells us to be renewed in the spirit of our mind as stated in Ephesians 4:23. To fulfill the mind of Christ and the language of Heaven you must step into the future beyond logic. The statement in Ephesian 2:6 tells us we are seated in Heavenly places in Christ Jesus. There is a depth of the anointing of Jesus to learn to walk in but only by changing the way you think. Deep is crying out to deep!

So, if you are going to win you must do it Gods way. To recover what has been taken from you takes effort. Even if you are the victim in a situation, and you are honest enough to admit you made mistakes. Forgive yourself, refocus on what you want. Then control what you think and speak to cause the process of removing the influence of a fall or failure.

It is a process of removing those things done to fail or fall, you must remind yourself of where you are going. As I remember an old radio statement, "You can't lose with the stuff I use." So, renew your mind, feed your vision and reaffirm your abilities. Choose your friends carefully, seriously!

It might take years to get somewhere in life, like accomplishments or reaching goals, education, employment, ministry. But then in a moment, it is gone by making wrong decisions or listening to wrong counsel. Your beginning started with a moment to get where you are at, so press in and start again and again and again. Winners never quit and quitters never win. Winning is inside out before it is ever outside in! You can do this! Jesus has faith in you (Galatians 2:20). So, don't quit. **You might have Fallen or Failed but Never Defeated!**

You have no limits unless you restrain yourself!

Chapter 10

Voice of Choice

In Psalms 19:12-14 the scripture is saying King David made a confessional plea in his relationship with God that is and should be a life-transforming issue for all of us.

> [12] "Who can understand his errors? cleanse thou me from secret faults. [13]Keep back thy servant also from presumptuous sins; let them not have dominion over me: then shall I be upright, and I shall be innocent from the great transgression. [14]Let the words of my mouth, and the meditation of my heart, be acceptable in thy sight, O LORD, my strength, and my redeemer."

Realizing that in your walking it is your talking. The way you carry yourself or present yourself is a language that can be heard by one's eyes only. For out of the abundance of the heart the mouth speaks is what Jesus said in Matthew 12:34. In the previous chapter on your Attitude, we shared the power of expression.

Many find themselves with passive-aggressiveness as we have a mindset or a conviction about an issue that can be expressed by our response before, we speak. Not all of us are willing to share what we think unless, or until we are provoked. Our dress or our body language has a voice and believe me it can be an unconscious statement never intended to be said.

We all speak many times without saying a word in a surprising situation or finding ourselves frustrated because of situations people initiated, also even dealing with cautious concern called fear. My physical expressions are a language. This is what we could list as involuntary reactions like involuntary muscles in our body. Growing up in life you find yourself put in a place of the **Voice of Choice**.

This voice speaks in volumes in how you respond to a challenge, a responsibility or a calamity. Your attitude, your words, your emotions in tears or anger or just a daze. Even the silent individual is speaking in some visible way.

Scratching one's hair, tapping with one's fingers, fidgety in some way, passive resistance or even speaking with one's eyes, and the eyes are known to be the window to one's subconscious or spirit. You have to make a choice in your life as stated in Deuteronomy 30:19-20. God went into covenant with Heaven and

Earth with the power of choice. The **Voice of Choice** is an expression that can change everything.

Not just your reactions, but your response in your words. What I want you to see more in this chapter is the power of your words, being physical or verbal. The old saying of the pen is mightier than the sword can be true. This is systematically true and circumstantially false.

In our relationship with others or our relationship with our creator and redeemer, we need to be conscious of the power of the tongue. Being like God is knowing that your words can change thoughts, actions, and results. You can speak without thinking just like you can breathe without thinking.

Working with teenagers can be a challenge in loving beyond their reaction to your words or influence. The one thing that used to bother me was the rolling of the eyes which was common in reluctant young ladies. Not wanting to be rebellious, but not really wanting to do what is asked of them.

I guess the rolling of the eyes is an inventory of is there an option here? I used to tease them and would say; I hope your eyes don't get stuck up there. Is love shown at its highest point in the rage of frustration or hindered?

The **Voice of Choice** should be the crying out of your conscience in times of temptation, frustration or even manipulation when coming from one's peers. Every person has three voices inside them; we all have the voice of our past, present, and future.

We also have the voice of our flesh, the voice of our soul (which is your mind, will, & emotions) and the voice of our spirit with the voice of the Holy Spirit in our spirit. Every human being is a living spirit, but to spend eternity in Heaven you must be born-again by asking and accepting Jesus Christ as Lord (Lord meaning supreme voice).

Every voice in you wants to control you except the voice of your spirit. When you have asked Jesus to live within you, to be your Lord. He never tries to control you or manipulate you or force you to follow his influence in your life. Body language is a voice, attitude is a voice, emotions speak loud as a voice, and even tears are a worldwide language that is easily understood around the world.

The definition of "Verbal" doesn't mean "spoken"; it merely indicates the use of words to communicate in whatever form. Most written and oral communication is verbal; some is non-verbal (grunts, sighs, laughter). A verbal expression does have a voice in all creation and it is different from human beings.

Animals have an expression in their own communications, in a type of culture in nature. Dogs bark, cat's meow, cows moo, goats baa, while birds chirp and sing, lions roar, etc. Animals have a voice and I would think, totally based on their nature, but not as a spirit being. Animals can be demon-possessed, realize demons want to come into bodies of humans or animals or objects, and all creation in general; demons want to control.

Remember Jesus wants you to follow his leadership and he does not drag, push or shove you or ever try to control you. Think about it, the **Voice of Choice** is your responsibility and authority once you have been redeemed by the blood of the Lamb of God. Romans 8:19 tells us of all creation is crying out for the manifestation of the Sons of God.

Even Jesus said of the rocks crying out to praise him if the people didn't. In Genesis 4:10 the voice of Able's blood cried out from the ground, because of Cain committing the act of murder when he killed his brother. In the book of 1 John, the Holy Spirit asks, "How can you say you love God and hate your brother?" Body language or how you treat others is a **Voice of Choice**. Jesus said; "But I say unto you, that every idle word that men shall speak, they shall give account thereof in the day of judgment." in Matthew 12:36.

I wonder if the words of Jesus still carry weight or is your words that carry life and death as Proverbs states, so covered by Grace that what you say has no accountability. But Galatians 6:7 tells us of what we sow is what we reap. My mother being a wonderful prayer warrior spoke a language that many others didn't know-how.

Something about praying mothers, demons fear; the bond between a child and its mother starts at conception. The language of love my mother and dad spoke they lived. My mother Anna White said, if you don't have anything good to say, say nothing. So, let us declare peoples future and quit talking about their past. Because love believes the best, and this is so hard for some as the memories speak loudly. Make a **Voice of Choice** and choose life, not death.

My mother when she was 14 was beaten by her Dad with an iron rod, simply because she asked, "why can't I go to school like other kids." This put her in bed for over a week. She had 7 siblings and she was the oldest that helped cook, clean and care for her brothers and sisters.

She chopped cotton in the cotton field while being raised working on a farm. My mother was an example of love; she cried and prayed all day it seemed. Then there were days she laughed and shouted praising God as the Glory of God filled the house.

At one time, I remember hearing my mother say to my Dad when he came home from work gripey, "Go Pray!" He did and the home was filled with peace and joy. I had a great wonderful childhood. My mother and dads life was a Voice of Choice, things were not always good, but love filled our home. I remember having just fried potatoes with tiny pieces of meat for dinner. My Dad working two jobs to take care of three boys and then came two girls.

The memories of other friends would leave their church to come to my house to sit at our family table. No matter the hardship, it was a voice of choice. My sister born with a cleft lip and cleft palate, the surgeries, the expenses, but still a house filled with praise and worship. We cannot choose our battles, but we can choose our response. The Voice of Choice comes from what God spoke in Deuteronomy 30:19-20, the covenant of power in words, with destiny based on Gods Word not mans.

Praying in tongues was common in our home. No matter what life did to you, what are you doing for others, you have the **Voice of Choice**. So, how do I declare the future of an unrepentant individual? Do I ignore or have a balance with a big personal issue? In

Mark 11:25 Jesus speaks these words, "And when ye stand praying, forgive, if ye have ought against any: that your Father also which is in heaven may forgive you your trespasses. 26 But if ye do not forgive, neither will your Father which is in heaven forgive your trespasses."

Your eternity is more important than your past or your pride or your hurt feelings. You are accountable to the **Voice of Choice!** Proverbs 18;21 says "life and death are in the power of the tongue." What I release in my mouth is powerful as stated in James 3:1-18 it can change the course of nature, words are powerful. Your life is filled with words, paragraphs and God even has your works in a book. I do not know of anyone worth me going to hell over, do you? So, speak your faith of I forgive them (call their name) and ask God to heal you of a wounded soul.

If I am in faith believing God for an answer to prayer, my **Voice of Choice** is not to repeat what circumstances are, as much as to declare what Gods word says as in 2 Corinthians 5:7, "For we walk by faith, not by sight." The words of doctors and lawyers can make your situation hopeless. You must choose to believe what God's word says.

I choose to speak what Gods word says about my moment and my situations. I stand on the promises of

God concerning the voice of my past, my present and my future. I declare as stated in Job 22:28 tells me, "Thou shalt also decree a thing, and it shall be established unto thee: and the light shall shine upon thy ways."

Mark 11:23-24 tells us to speak to the mountain and believe your words meaning your **Voice of Choice** makes the obstacles or resistance to Gods word to be removed and cast into the sea. Remember your attitude is a voice, it is your faith in action. Speaking what God says creates change.

That is why Joshua 1:8 is serious to live by, the sea of forgetfulness as God cast our sins into as stated in Micah 7:19 "He will turn again; he will have compassion upon us; he will subdue our iniquities; and thou wilt cast all their sins into the depths of the sea."

Responding and addressing an attack of the enemy is not a voice of despair, but of violence as stated in Matthew 11:22 that "the kingdom of heaven suffers violence and the violent take it by force." It is an attitude that has body language that speaks and displays expression. There is no walking in love or forgiveness to what you should ever express toward the Devil and what he and his demons are trying to do to you, or anyone in your family.

In Ephesians 6:10-19, the Spirit of God tells us we wrestle not against flesh and blood, but principalities and powers of darkness. The reference of armor is there for defense, as the shield of faith, and the helmet of salvation, and the breastplate of righteousness, and the belt of truth, but the part of attack being the offense is the sword of the Spirit which is the word of God. We must choose the **Voice of Choice** to win because we are praying always in the Spirit as stated in verse 18 of Ephesians 6. An attitude or **voice of choice** does not have to be loud as much as peaceful and confident. Violent is not passive but positional to attack.

We as believers are not on defense but offense. We are as God said to Gideon in Judges 7:9, we are going into the enemies camp to take back what has been taken from us. Psalms 107:2 says "Let the redeemed of the Lord say so."

Galatians 3:13,14 tells me "I am redeemed from sin, sickness, and poverty and set free from the powers and influence of the darkness." How you see yourself in the mirror is the presentation of external, but how your spirit responds is greater than what you can see, being it is internal.

In high school, I read a story that has really stuck with me. The story was about three men who were thieves who wanted to rob a warehouse and to do so the plan was two went inside the building, while one stayed outside in a police uniform to act like the place was guarded. The uniformed officer was there as a phycological deterrent, his clothes spoke a language everyone wanted to hear.

As the two robbers were inside to steal, the one was outside as a police officer walking and standing around whistling. He stopped and helped a lady across the street, helped a child retrieved a cat from a tree, waved at people and being respectful and courteous. He really was enjoying the people and the response of respect he was given. As the two thieves were climbing over the wall from robbing the warehouse. The third man stopped and saw them and blew the whistle and cried out stop in the name of the law. Other policemen came on the chase as the third thief was in on his partners' arrest.

The emphasis of the story was that "clothes make the man." When the outside and the inside of you meet, you become the call and destiny of your birth. An eye conversation can be carried on from a distance, what you see, what you hear and what you think is expressed in what you see. It is like, if you didn't see it, you really didn't hear it.

Perception, interpretation, and illumination are the languages of the eyes. Really what you see is not always what you get. Judging a book by its color does not speak the content. But eye language is a developed practice of putting a puzzle together. Most people start a puzzle with the limits and borders, but God has no limits, and he starts putting the picture of your life together from the middle of your heart.

Remember your **Voice of Choice** is out of the abundance of the heart the mouth shall speak. Luke 6:45 tells us of the voice within one's self. "A good man out of the good treasure of his heart bringeth forth that which is good; and an evil man out of the evil treasure of his heart bringeth forth that which is evil: for of the abundance of the heart his mouth speaks."

In Proverbs 18:21 the wisdom of God shares that "Death and life [are] in the power of the tongue: and they that love it shall eat the fruit thereof. Peter tells us in 1 Peter 3:10, "For he that will love life, and see good days, let him refrain his tongue from speaking evil, and his lips that they speak no guile: We find world peace or times of war hinge on the words of leaders as stated in James chapter 3, the whole chapter gives detail of the power of the tongue. This is not just about the voice of your flesh but charting the course of your nature and destiny is in your words.

James 3:1-18

1 My brethren, be not many masters, knowing that we shall receive the greater condemnation.

2 For in many things we offend all. If any man offend not in word, the same is a perfect man, and able also to bridle the whole body.

3 Behold, we put bits in the horses' mouths, that they may obey us; and we turn about their whole body.

4 Behold also the ships, which though they be so great, and are driven of fierce winds, yet are they turned about with a very small helm, whithersoever the governor list.

5 Even so the tongue is a little member, and boast great things. Behold, how great a matter a little fire kindles!

6 And the tongue is a fire, a world of iniquity: so is the tongue among our members, that it defiles the whole body, and sets on fire the course of nature; and it is set on fire of hell.

7 For every kind of beasts, and of birds, and of serpents, and of things in the sea, is tamed, and hath been tamed of mankind:

8 But the tongue can no man tame; it is an unruly evil, full of deadly poison.

9 Therewith bless we God, even the Father; and therewith curse we men, which are made after the similitude of God.

10 Out of the same mouth proceeds blessing and cursing. My brethren, these things ought not so to be.

11 Doth a fountain send forth at the same place sweet water and bitter?

12 Can the fig tree, my brethren, bear olive berries? either a vine, figs? so can no fountain both yield salt water and fresh.

13 Who is a wise man and endued with knowledge among you? let him shew out of a good conversation his works with meekness of wisdom.

14 But if ye have bitter envying and strife in your hearts, glory not, and lie not against the truth.

15 This wisdom descends not from above, but is earthly, sensual, devilish.

16 For where envying and strife is, there is confusion and every evil work.

17 But the wisdom that is from above is first pure, then peaceable, gentle, and easy to be intreated, full of mercy and good fruits, without partiality, and without hypocrisy.

18 And the fruit of righteousness is sown in peace of them that make peace.

Remember the Voice of Choice is in the power of your words, no matter what language you speak. Your clothes speak, your attitude and actions speak. Your face speaks and I remind you of my Dads words of "Boy don't you dare talk to me with that look."

Jesus is the Prince of Peace as stated in Isaiah 9:6-7 of His government there is no end. Your submission to His influence in your life, speaks by the level of peace you walk and live in. 1 John 5:14 tells us about confidence in prayer, is a result of a relationship with the Spirit of God. The following verses are for the purpose of the power of the **Voice of Choice**.

If you think like the world, you will talk like the world. To learn the language of Heaven is to learn the ways of God. So, "study that you may show yourself approved of God" 2 Timothy 2:15.

1. Proverbs 15:1 - A soft answer turns away wrath: but grievous words stir up anger.

2. Ephesians 4:29 - Let no corrupt communication proceed out of your mouth, but that which is good to the use of edifying, that it may minister grace unto the hearers.

3. Psalms 118:5 - I called upon the LORD in distress: the LORD answered me, [and set me] in a large place.

4. Psalms 141:3 - Set a watch, O LORD, before my mouth; keep the door of my lips.

5. James 1:26 - If any man among you seem to be religious, and bridles not his tongue, but deceives his own heart, this man's religion [is] vain.

6. Proverbs 10:19 - In the multitude of words is foolishness: but he that refrains his lips [is] wise.

7. Proverbs 15:28 - The heart of the righteous studies to answer: but the mouth of the wicked pours out evil things.

8. Proverbs 12:18 - There is he that speaks like the piercings of a sword, stabbing: but the tongue of the wise [is] health.

9. Psalms 19:14 - Let the words of my mouth, and the meditation of my heart, be acceptable in thy sight, O LORD, my strength, and my redeemer.

10. Proverbs 15:4 - A wholesome tongue [is] a tree of life: but perverseness therein [is] a breach in the spirit.

11. James 1:19 - Wherefore, my beloved brethren, let every man be swift to hear, slow to speak, slow to wrath:

12. Philippians 2:14 - Do all things without murmurings and strife:

13. Proverbs 13:3 - He that keeps his mouth keeps his life: [but] he that opens wide his lips shall have destruction.

The **Voice of Choice** goes all the way to Deuteronomy 30:19,20 " The covenant that God made with Heaven and Earth. You have the ability to change lives while helping people. But you cannot give what you do not have. Learn the ways of God that you might do His mighty acts. Below are the words of a traditional Hymnal that has stood the test of time. Realize that music has words and words are filled with life or death. I pray you never leave your X in Texas or that you never have a poker face. As Jesus said that they may know you are his disciples because you have love for one another. Hope is expectancy that is one reason I love this song.

Choice is the creator of change!

"My Hope is Built on Nothing Less"
by Edward Mote, 1797-1874

1. My hope is built on nothing less
Than Jesus' blood and righteousness;
I dare not trust the sweetest frame,
But wholly lean on Jesus' name.
On Christ, the solid Rock, I stand;
All other ground is sinking sand.

2. When darkness veils His lovely face,
I rest on His unchanging grace;
In every high and stormy gale
My anchor holds within the veil.
On Christ, the solid Rock, I stand;
All other ground is sinking sand.

3. His oath, His covenant, and blood
Support me in the whelming flood;
When every earthly prop gives way,
He then is all my Hope and Stay.
On Christ, the solid Rock, I stand;
All other ground is sinking sand.

4. When He shall come with trumpet sound,
Oh, may I then in Him be found,
Clothed in His righteousness alone,
Faultless to stand before the throne!
On Christ, the solid Rock, I stand;
All other ground is sinking sand.

Kathryn Kuhlman made the statement "The choice you make can shake the world for God." As stated in another chapter, "To be or not to be, that is the question." To not make a choice is making a choice. If you live off excuses, you can die because of the reasons. You must not allow confusion to control your choices. The Voice of Choice will be made for you by circumstances if you do not think for yourself. God gave you the ultimate answer and that starts and ends with Jesus. I love this old song,

"I found the answer, I've learned to pray, with
faith to guild me along the way. The sun is
shining for me each day, I've found the answer.
I've learned to pray."

God only requires out of us what he has given us the ability to do.

Joshua 24:15 15But if serving the LORD seems undesirable to you, then choose for yourselves this day whom you will serve, whether the gods your ancestors served beyond the Euphrates or the gods of the Amorites, in whose land you are living. **But as for me and my household, we will serve the LORD."** The **Voice of Choice** is what will surface under the pressure of life. Commitment is a preference of what you believe and what you are. 2 Chronicles 15:7 Be strong therefore and let not your hands be weak; for your work shall be rewarded.

The dreams of tomorrow can be filled by the choices of today.

There is something called the process of elimination, it is a filtering process of what you accept and what you reject. This is the power of choice. Choice is the creator of change and some things in life you can conquer with no effort, but only by the complicated power of choice will you make the right decisions. Being a parent does not make you guilty of how your children turned out. When you have done your part with all the purity of your heart, let not their stray from the way have final say in your heart. For the seed of harvest, you will begin to see, as they grow older, they will begin to be the harvest you desired to see. Acts 16:31 says "And they said, believe on the Lord Jesus Christ, and thou shalt be saved, and thy whole house." What you did may not have been perfect, but if you tried to love them the way you wanted to be loved. God will cause them to honor you.

Do what's right even when there is pressure to compromise? Remember what you compromise to get, you will ultimately lose. In all that you know and do, your conscience is the choice of your eternity, so walk, not run and seek God for understanding on how you follow and who, then you can lead by example, for all eyes are on you! **Voice of Choice.**

> Words can be short... but the meaning long... life is like the weather the changes continue on... my fortitude is beyond logic because it's dependent on His Grace and without His Mercy some things would not take place... the battle may be the Lords but the responsibility of victory is mine... in the mist of each battle my attitude is what should shine... at times there is remorse for what I want things to be... having just one word in due season defies the logic of what I cannot see...

So, I have given you ten phrases that you can make a difference in your life with.

Always tell the Truth

Love is Considerate

Be Responsible

Have Integrity

Pursue Excellence

To Your Own Self Be True

Control Your Attitude

Being Safe is Wisdom

Never Defeated

Voice of Choice

Memorize, Meditate and Apply yourself to see God work in your life! **Remember you may be the only Bible that some people read, so act like Jesus!**

Pass this book on to others to let them experience this teaching that will change their lives.

Your greatest investment is in you!

If you are not born again; You need Jesus!

Romans 10:13 "For whosoever shall call upon the name of the Lord shall be saved."

Pray with me;

Jesus come in my heart. I believe you are the son of God; I believe you were born of a virgin, and you died on a cross, and God raised you from the dead. I believe you are alive, and I ask you Jesus for you to open my eyes to understand, and come live in my heart, that I may learn your ways to do your acts in sharing your love. Thank you, Jesus, for saving me. Now I ask that you fill me with the Holy Spirit, that I may speak the language of Heaven. Amen.

Welcome to the Family of God.

Now tell someone you have asked Jesus to come in your heart, that now He is your Lord and Savior.

DR. MARK D. WHITE
EXPRESSING THE FATHER'S HEART

Mark D. White was raised an Assembly of God pastor's son and started preaching at the age of 15. In 1978 he graduated from Kenneth E. Hagin's Rhema Bible Training Center in Tulsa, Oklahoma. Since then he has been an associate pastor of two churches and has pastored three. Mark also holds a Doctorate from Saint Thomas University and a BS/BM from the University of Phoenix. Mark has authored and published three books.

Mark travels extensively throughout the United States and travels Internationally, ministering the Word of God by precept and example. His having over 47 years of active experience in ministry, gives place to the workings of the Holy Spirit in the lives of the believers and unbelievers. Mark's insight and practical understanding in the spirit, makes room for him to operate in the Prophet's office with a Pastor's heart. There is a strong tangible anointing upon him, which gives place to the open move of the Holy Spirit in edifying and comforting the local church.

Mark has a reputation for balanced teaching and preaching with compassion for the heart of the people. Homes are restored, blind eyes are opened, deaf ears are healed, cancer disappears, cataracts are removed, and broken hearts are mended. The Word of God is preached with signs following. Miracles and Healings happen in every service. It is Mark's desire to serve the purpose of each and every local church and ministry.

www.markwhite.tv
www.rapha.us

Email address – rapha@gmx.us
Donations: www.paypal.me/markdwhite

Other books written by Dr. Mark D. White

Your Identity
The Thumbprint of God

Change your today, while creating tomorrow. Speak what God says and let the fruit of your lips come from the seed of your thoughts. You are one of the best investments you could ever make in your lifetime. Remember that what you feed grows and what you starve dies. You are the Thumbprint of God, Let Him finish His work in you; seek Him as He is seeking you. The potter; being God is still shaping you to fulfill your destiny.

Time the Unfound Friend

Time is the most powerful force on earth. Every nation and leader submits to the power of time. In business, politics or everyday life, all plans and desires are under the influence of time. It seems that no one can find time to invest in their moment, everyone's eternity hinges on it. In the Emergency Room or the field of battle, choices are made by prior preparation. To learn how to succeed, one learns how to overcome. You are at the greatest place of your life. So, look for Time the Unfound Friend and if you work together, changes will take place. You can make a difference around the world starting right now!

**What is important, is not how
you leave this earth; as much
as how you enter eternity.**